THROUGH AFRICAN EYES

VOLUME 2

THROUGH AFRICAN EYES

COMPILED BY

PAUL EDWARDS

*Lecturer in English Literature in the
University of Edinburgh*

VOLUME 2

CAMBRIDGE
AT THE UNIVERSITY PRESS
1966

PUBLISHED BY
THE SYNDICS OF THE CAMBRIDGE UNIVERSITY PRESS

Bentley House, 200 Euston Road, London, N.W. 1
American Branch: 32 East 57th Street, New York, N.Y. 10022
West African Office: P.M.B. 5181, Ibadan, Nigeria

Printed in Great Britain at the University Printing House, Cambridge
(Brooke Crutchley, University Printer)

CONTENTS

v

CONTENTS

ACKNOWLEDGEMENTS

For permission to quote copyright material, acknowledgement is made to the following: Messrs Allen and Unwin (Ajao, *On the Tiger's Back*); Messrs Collins (Bloom, *Episode*; Ike, *Toads for Supper*); Messrs André Deutsch (Ghali, *Beer in the Snooker Club*); Messrs Faber and Faber (Frobenius and Fox, *African Genesis*); Messrs John Farquharson (Abrahams, *Tell Freedom*); Messrs Robert Hale (Atiyah, *Black Vanguard*); Messrs Harrap (Dean, *Umbala*); Messrs Heinemann (Achebe, *Things Fall Apart*); Heinemann Educational Books (Ngugi, *Weep Not, Child*); The Hogarth Press (Plomer, *Ula Masonda*); Messrs Hutchinson (Ekwensi, *Jagua Nana*); Messrs Macgibbon and Kee (Nicol, *Always the Best*); Messrs Frederick Muller (Beti, *Mission to Kala*) the Oxford University Press under the auspices of the International African Institute (Mofolo, *Chaka, An Historical Romance*); Messrs Secker and Warburg (Kenyatta, *Facing Mount Kenya*); the United Society for the Propagation of the Gospel (Kilekwa, *Slave Boy to Priest*); Messrs Weidenfeld and Nicolson (Charhadi, *A Life Full of Holes*).

ABIOSEH NICOL

SIERRA LEONE

Always the Best

From *Always the Best* (in *Alienation*, ed. T. O'Keefe). Abioseh
Nicol describes a crucial period in his life, the few months before
he left Freetown with a scholarship to Cambridge. He was to go on
to a distinguished career, but here he is only an eighteen-year-old
clerk, just out of school, with all his ambitions still to be realized.

It had been clear to me from the age of ten that I would one
day visit Britain. I had overheard a friend saying to my father
in West Africa that he should begin to think seriously of giving
his two sons a profession. This, in West African English,
meant sending them to Britain to study for one of the learned
professions, Medicine or Law, because these gave a man
dignity, independence and financial reward. My father thought
it would be better to do Science instead because, he explained
vaguely, these were modern times.

By the age of eighteen, a school-friend and I practically
knew the contents of the prospectuses of all the Universities
in Great Britain and most of the Negro Universities in America.
He was more interested in the latter, as he held radical views
and felt America gave more in the way of resourcefulness; he
had also a practical reason: his mother was a widow and he
had to depend on his own savings for further education, and
so the prospect of working one's way through College, which
was possible in the States and not in Britain, was very appeal-
ing. I much preferred the idea of Britain. I had secretly read
the diary kept by my father when he was in London and
prosaic names like Dulwich, Westminster Abbey, and St
Pancras were shot through for me with unutterable romance.

My brother and I were in the Civil Service but he had been
transferred to another town. So in the evening I would stroll

down the road to my friend and converse about entrance requirements, degree courses, and the colours of hoods. Over lemonade, in the blackout of the early years of the war, we discussed Universities with the eagerness of men discussing horses and women.

The courses we wanted to do were not taken in the small local College and in any case we wanted to get away. Sometimes I wandered down to the harbour and looked far into the horizon in the direction in which Britain lay. There in that country they said you could actually meet the people who wrote books, actually hear them speak, touch them...

Every mail boat day some of us rushed to the bookshop with saved-up salaries or pocket money and bought Penguins, Pelicans and cheap editions of books, read through them during the day in between typing and filing letters at the office, or teaching at School, and in the evenings after finishing our Correspondence Course lessons.

The war was on and our parents refused to let us go. In desperation I tried to join the R.A.F., was accepted, started packing, then failed the medicals through bad eyesight. By that time an influx of Europeans (as the British are called in West Africa) had been brought in by the war. Trade Union organizers, accountants, scientists, young men just down from the Universities, British Council people, soldiers and airmen. Before the war the resident European population, whether civil servants, traders or missionaries, kept very much to themselves after duty hours. There was no colour prejudice as such because they simply did not mix and so were not missed. Their influence on the local population in towns was remote, impersonal, and exerted only by a very small but devoted fraction who were mostly, but not entirely, in the educational service. Those who came during the war crashed through the barriers. They had no white man's burden or stiff protocol to maintain. In fairness it must be added that they were only there temporarily. They had, therefore, no necessity to keep the distance thought necessary if a small, largely unarmed, group of administrators were asked to maintain law and order among millions in Asia or Africa. Thus it was easy for the new ones to make friends. I got to know four or five very well and was in and out of their Nissen huts and bungalows looking at their books, listening to their gramophone records, absorbing information about Britain with glittering eyes, basking in their obvious kindness and affection. They once said that apart from servants and junior clerks they found it very difficult to meet any educated Africans; so I agreed to arrange some contact. We decided to give a party and I asked some friends in my own social class. They were people who had been to local grammar schools and colleges, men and women, all, of course, West Africans. The evening of the party arrived and I bustled around happily. One of the guests drew me aside, slightly puzzled by my familiarity with our British hosts.

'Who is paying for this party? Government? The Secret Service? Or what?'

'It's just a social party,' I replied.

'Are you working for a scholarship or an M.B.E. or promotion?'

'I am working for nothing. They just want to meet us and I think it is worthwhile mixing. They are nice people and good friends.'

'I don't think we gain much by mixing with them, you know,' he said, and sipping neat whisky, returned thoughtfully to a corner. Only two of the female guests had turned up, both were English; one the wife of a young and brilliant administrative officer, the other something to do with Social Welfare. We were expecting the other eight, who were Africans.

'What has happened to them?' one of our hosts asked me. I borrowed a car and went off to look for them. The first was the daughter of an old friend of my father, both retired Civil Servants. I found she had not yet even changed.

'Papa says I should not go!'

'Why?' Just then Papa came downstairs in his braces and asked me directly if my father knew I was giving this party— I said he did not know, I had not asked him. After bringing us up with great strictness until the age of sixteen my father had left us to our own devices. My interrogator persisted. Did my father know I was giving a party with white men? This was the first time I had heard my British friends described so bluntly; I had never quite thought of them as that after the first few weeks.

'No, he did not know,' I answered.

'Ah, I thought not.' He seemed satisfied. Then he continued gravely.

'Do you think my daughter is a harlot to go and mix with white men? They only want one thing out of women, those people. Have you no shame! Since when have you, a young man from a good home, started finding women for white men? I should have thought you knew better!'

He stomped off upstairs. I left.

The other parents gave varying excuses but they all had the same idea. I managed to get four of my invited guests to come by promising I would take them home myself soon after midnight. 'I had never thought of this matter of transport,' one of our British hosts happily said, when I turned up successful and unhappy with the four girls, who were quite amused for different reasons.

'We must organize things better next time,' he ended, waltzing off with one.

My British friends persuaded me to go to one of the older Universities, adding vaguely that they thought I was the type. I discussed this with my compatriots and my father. They did not believe serious students went to Oxford and Cambridge.

People only went there for the social life and the boat race, according to them. London, Edinburgh, Newcastle, those were places people go to for hard study and work, my father said; he had studied in London himself. 'Besides,' he added, 'You are not the only one in the family and I cannot spend everything on you. Name me a single successful person here who has been to Oxford or Cambridge.'

There were only four Africans who had been to Oxford that I knew, none who had been to Cambridge; and by no stretch of the imagination could they have been described as successful in the sense my father meant.

At last, one day he put on his stiff white collar, bow tie, sun helmet, well-pressed suit and went off to see the local Director of Education. Like most old Africans who had been long in the service of the British Government, he had a great faith in the word of senior British civil servants, whose integrity he believed to be unshakable. He discussed my education with him. The battle was lost before he started. The Director was an old Oxford pre-1914 man. I had filled in time working for him occasionally as a clerk, and he had once told me how daring undergraduates in his time read Swinburne and believed in him.

'I am sure he should go to Oxford or Cambridge, probably the latter as he is interested in science.'

'It is expensive in those places,' my father said, 'Only very rich people go there.'

'No, not necessarily. I went to a provincial Grammar School myself and won an exhibition to Oxford.'

He paused delicately, wondering whether his offer would hurt my father's feelings. He need not have worried.

'I believe in your son and I do not want you to send him just anywhere. We have got some money which we have not used at all in the department and we can let him have it.'

'At what rate of interest?' my father asked after a while.

I knew after being defeated into a more expensive University he would balance in his mind whether he should sell property.

'No, it is not a loan, I shall see that he has it outright without any bond at all. I believe in him and whatever he does in the future will reflect good on his country. Let him go to Cambridge, let him have the best. Always the best.'

Outside my father gravely repeated the conversation and pointed out to me again that in this, I could see, if I was willing, the greatness of the British. 'That Director said to me, "Let him have the best, always the best." He had no need to, but he said so; "Always the best!"'

I was not particularly moved. 'It is his job,' I said. 'Besides, that is what the money is there for. It is not his, it is our money that we pay in taxes. And how does he know that Oxford and Cambridge are the best, he has never been elsewhere.'

My father turned round furiously on me. 'That is your trouble, you of the younger generation, you are ungrateful. That's it! Ingratitude! I have seen the rubbish you pack on your bookshelves. Socialism, politics, godlessness, Thinker's Library. You waste your time going to political meetings and talking about nationalism and freedom. Freedom, indeed. Those nationalist friends of yours have not done a day's honest work in their lives. I have heard of the anti-British rubbish you and your friends talk about. Where would you and your useless crowd be without the British? Where?'

I was upset. In the past few months every conversation with my father ended in an argument or a quarrel; we seemed then always to see things from such different points of view. He called a taxi and went off home. I wandered off sadly in the direction of a library. I met my disbelieving friend from the party. He congratulated me on my good news. Although it was only an hour old, I was not surprised that he knew. Nothing was secret in the tropics; a clerk or messenger had probably been listening at the keyhole of the Director's office.

'My God,' he said, waving his arms, 'Cambridge and all expenses paid. Cambridge, where all the poets and statesmen go! They are rewarding your father, fine old pensioner who served them in the Nigerian Service for thirty years. They are rewarding your grandfather, fine old soldier who fought for them until they gave him a sword to drag and many medals.'

He thrust his head forward and smiled mockingly. He raised his voice in mimicry.

'Dear Abioseh; let him have the best, always the best.'

I turned and walked away heavily and sadly.

JOMO KENYATTA

KENYA

An African Education

From *Facing Mount Kenya*. Jomo Kenyatta draws a contrast between European and Gikuyu education: the first, he says, aims at the development of the individual even at the expense of society, the second at the blending of the individual with his group. There are a number of general truths here, but I think you should be prepared, after reading it, to discuss it in some detail. For example, Kenyatta says that in Europe 'freedom of personality is the highest good, and co-ordination with other people...something accidental', but could the complex democratic societies of Europe have developed had this been wholly true? Will the modern African state, under modern economic conditions, find it any easier than Europe or America to preserve the close ties of family or village? Where local ties are strong, for instance in the village, tribe or family, is it possible that this might even hinder the growth of stability in the larger society of the nation?

Every clan and family has its heroes, *njamba*, past and present. Their heroic deeds are related and their praises sung round the fire of an evening. This is one of the methods of instilling ambition and a sense of duty into the hearts of the growing generation. The child or youth who does not give the service demanded of his position will be told 'you are not one of the family of So-and-so' (*ndore wa mbari ya ng'ania* or *ndotoketie mbari ya ng'ania*). The good old days before the advent of the Europeans are lauded to the skies. These were the days of wars and national pride, of heroes and great leaders of the dance, days when men went together to plunder, when they were all brave, and no man deserted his friend; their motto was '*Njamba egoaga na erea enge*,' which means, 'Together we win or die'. Of course, since the Gikuyu are not a society of angels, adherence to these social rules depends on the morale and courage of individuals.

The selfish or self-regarding man has no name or reputation in the Gikuyu community. An individualist is looked upon with suspicion and is given a nickname of *mwebongia*, one who works only for himself and is likely to end up as a wizard. He may lack assistance when he needs it. He cannot expect that everything he does will prosper, for the weight of opinion makes him feel his crime against society. Religious sanction works against him, too, for Gikuyu religion is always on the side of solidarity. The aged and weak are under the special protection of the ancestral spirits, and they are never far away from home. Thus the labour of the hands, the begetting of children, the amassing of wealth in the form of land, cattle, sheep and goats are, just as much as religious ceremonies, matters of family and clan settlement.

In the Gikuyu community there is no really individual affair, for everything has a moral and social reference. The habit of corporate effort is but the other side of corporate ownership; and corporate responsibility is illustrated in corporate work no less than in corporate sacrifice and prayer.

In spite of the foreign elements which work against many of the Gikuyu institutions and the desire to implant the system of wholesale Westernization, this system of mutual help and the tribal solidarity in social services, political and economic activities are still maintained by the large majority of the Gikuyu people. It is less practised among those Gikuyu who have been Europeanized or detribalized. The rest of the community look upon these people as mischief-makers and breakers of the tribal traditions, and the general disgusted cry is heard: '*Mothongo ne athogonjire borori*,' i.e. the white man had spoiled and disgraced our country.

The rising generation is trained in beliefs and customs necessary to the self-maintenance of the tribe and interrelation with the neighbouring tribes. The fundamental needs of reproduction, extraction of food from the environment, and social solidarity are recognized and met. The tribal society not only maintains its existence, but secures the continuity of its distinctive features over against other tribes. We have therefore to ask ourselves whether a system of education which proves so successful in realizing its particular objectives may not have some valuable suggestion to offer or advice to give the European whose assumed task it is in these days to provide Western education for the African.

The first and most obvious principle of educational value which we see in the Gikuyu system of education is that the instruction is always applied to an individual concrete situation; behaviour is taught in relation to some particular person. Whereas in Europe and America schools provide courses in moral instruction or citizenship, the African is taught how to behave to father or mother, grandparents, and to other members of the kinship group, paternal or maternal. Whereas European schools in Africa provide training in nature study, woodwork, animal husbandry, etc., much of which is taught by general class instruction, the tribal method is to teach the names of particular plants, the use of different trees, or the management of a particular herd of sheep and goats or cattle. After this the child is left free to develop his own initiative by experiments and through trial and error to acquire proficiency.

The striking thing in the Gikuyu system of education, and the feature which most sharply distinguishes it from the European system of education, is the primary place given to personal relations. Each official statement of educational policy repeats this well-worn declaration that the aim of education must be the building of character and not the mere acquisition of knowledge. But European practice falls short of this principle; knowledge is the dominating objective in the European method of teaching in Africa as a whole and, as long as exams rule, it is hard to see how anything else can be given primary importance. While the Westerner asserts that character formation is the chief thing, he forgets that character is formed primarily through relations with other people, and that there is really no other way in which it can grow. Europeans assume that, given the right knowledge and ideas, personal relations can be left largely to take care of themselves, and this is perhaps the most fundamental difference in outlook between Africans and Europeans. It can be safely said that, in the European system of education, school co-ordination, and especially social subordination, marriage, the family, the school, vocation, relation of people to the State, etc., are all regarded as things which have grown up of themselves, as historical forms which, however, are always capable, as such, of change, and over which the free man, namely, the personality, must have authority. For freedom of personality is the highest good, and co-ordination with other people and especially mutual subordination are on the contrary something accidental. Here it is worth while to ask a question which seems very pertinent to our subject: 'If it is true that the European system of education aims at individuality, is it then to be wondered at that Europeans educated in this way have some difficulty in finding the right place for the organic tribal relationships of the Africans?' We may sum it up by saying that to the Europeans 'Individuality is the ideal of life,' to the Africans the ideal is the right relations with, and behaviour to, other people. No doubt education philosophy can make a higher synthesis in which these two great truths are one, but the fact remains that while the Europeans place the emphasis on one side the Africans place it on the other.

HARRY DEAN
U.S.A.

A Mixed Marriage, 1782

From *Umbala*. Harry Dean was an American, but there is some justification for including him in this anthology. His grandfather on his mother's side was the famous negro seafarer Paul Cuffee, and his father's family came originally from Morocco. 'I am an African and proud of it,' he wrote, 'There is not a drop of white blood in my veins.'

He was born in 1864, and *Umbala* describes his adventurous life as a sailor. One of these adventures was an attempt to set up an independent 'Ethiopian Empire', as he called it, in Pondoland, South Africa, and it was there that he came across this story, and the descendants of the people involved in it.

In the year 1782 the *Grosvenor*, an East Indiaman homeward bound from Ceylon, was wrecked off the south-east coast of Africa. She was reported to have had one million pounds sterling aboard, and silver coins are still picked up on the beach in the vicinity of the wreck. As in the case of hundreds of other ancient disasters, so many myths have sprung up surrounding it that it is hard to separate the truth from the fiction. Several of the accounts, palpably false, tell of terrible hardships endured by these people. Dozens of old romancers posing as historians have embellished the tale, until it is generally believed that the survivors were forced to walk hundreds of miles through a burning, desert-like country, subsisting almost entirely on carrion, being beaten, robbed, and (in the case of the women) carried away by the natives, escaping the attacks of wild animals only by miracle, and, with the exception of a mere handful, dying before they reached the Cape.

As a matter of fact, the ship was wrecked some twenty-five miles from what is now Port St John's, on the coast of Pondoland, where the country was so fertile and the food so plentiful that a baby could have survived. As for the natives, knowing them as I do, I have every reason to believe that they helped these unfortunate men and women.

I was at Kow Kenny over a century after the disaster when I learned of an old woman, living some fifteen miles from the kraal, who, according to all reports, had a skin almost as white as that of an English lady. A hundred stories centred about her. Some of the natives thought she was a goddess and had come on wings, like a seagull, many years before. Some said that she was the daughter of the daughter of a castaway.

It came to my mind that she might be a descendant of one of the survivors from the *Grosvenor*. I was determined to look into the matter. With Emtinso to guide me, I set forth one morning, and at last arrived at a neat stone house lying in a pleasant valley. A girl of perhaps fourteen met us at the door. Her skin was dark brown, but it seemed to me that there was a slightly Anglo-Saxon cast to her features. Emtinso spoke to her in Pondo, explaining something of the nature of our visit. She replied in the same musical tongue in which he had addressed her.

'What does she say, Emtinso?' I asked.

To my great surprise the girl herself answered, and in English. 'I said that Grandmother is at home if you wish to see her,' she explained.

We were led into a bright little room, and there, before an open window, with the sunshine falling upon her, sat the lady of whom we had heard. Rumour had not exaggerated the whiteness of her skin nor the Caucasian mould of her face. She was a woman of sixty-five or seventy, white-haired, proud in bearing, and soft-spoken. As in the case of her grand-daughter, she used both English and Pondo.

I had not been mistaken in my surmise. This old woman's mother's mother had been aboard the *Grosvenor* on that ill-fated trip. At our request she told the story as it had come down by word of mouth. Occasionally a quaint word pointed to the fact that not only the story, but the use of the language as well, had been handed from mother to daughter. There was remarkably little admixture of native or Boer words and phrases. These people had, in a manner, lived to themselves.

I had expected her story to be quite unlike the written accounts of the wreck, and in this I was not disappointed. She spoke as if the castaways had actually liked the fertile shores upon which they had been thrown, and, while they had always dreamed of some day returning to England, they had settled in Pondoland rather than attempt the journey to the Cape.

She seemed to delight in recounting the story, and her words carried us back to the decks of the *Grosvenor*. Mary Cartwright was twenty-two that year, and a widow of less than two months. She had accompanied her husband to India, for his regiment had been detailed for foreign service shortly after their marriage, and they could neither of them bear the thought of parting. She had found the country so unlike England that she had been homesick for Devonshire, but the pleasure of being near her young husband had outweighed all other considerations.

They had been married a little less than a year when he was brought in one day sick with fever. And though she nursed him day and night, he at last died, leaving her alone in a foreign country. Thus it was that she took passage on the *Grosvenor*, East Indiaman, and in 1782 was wrecked on the south-east coast of Africa. When the ship had gone aground the passengers had rushed to the deck in a panic. The surf was so high that all the attempts to launch lifeboats had been futile. A bold swimmer had at last carried a life-line to shore, and over this all but one made their way to safety. The one who perished was the cook's mate, who had been so drunk that he had refused to leave the ship.

Little had been salvaged. The small hoard of provisions was divided among the survivors, and they had set out toward the distant Cape, unaware of their true position or of the difficulties they were about to encounter. They followed the coast, and were able to supplement their inadequate stores by gathering shellfish from the sea and picking fruits and berries, which they saw the birds eat freely, from the trees and bushes that grew on every hillside. At night they built great fires, more to keep up their courage than to protect them from wild animals, for they were in little danger on that score. During the day they carried lighted firebrands with them, for they had been able to salvage but one poor flint and steel from the wreck.

At first the women and children had been able to keep up. The men had assisted them wherever the country was rough. At last, however, as they were increasingly aware of their distance from civilization, it was decided that all the sailors and most of the men should go on ahead and the women and children follow at their own pace. The hope was to reach help quickly and send a rescue-party to assist the women and children. After a sad leave-taking the men went forward, giving more of the provisions than they could easily spare to those who were to follow them on their journey.

Two days later the women came to a river so wide and so deep that they were unable to cross it in any manner whatsoever. The men had either been able to swim it or had found native craft of some description to carry them across. The women were less fortunate, and found the stream a perfect barrier against further progress.

The old woman paused a moment, smiled, and gazed out of the window. 'My grandmother,' she said, 'never heard the fate of those who went ahead. I have heard stories of their journey which in many respects are to be doubted. It is said that on the sixth day after their parting with the women they ran out of provisions. They had come upon a region so dry and so barren that they could find no food wherewith to nourish their bodies, nor water wherewith they might quench their thirst. These accounts tell how they discovered thrown up upon the shore a dead seal, which they tore to pieces like wild beasts in their desire for food. It is stated that they walked weary miles with parched tongues, even drinking the sea-water and worse. The mussels which they gathered here were so salt that they only increased their agony. Most doubtful of all are those parts of the stories which relate to the brutality of the natives. My grandmother's story tells of nothing but kindness at the hands of the natives.

'But of the women who were left behind...' She pictured for us the crude camp these women made, waiting day after day for the rescue-party which never came. Mary Cartwright, alone with her thoughts, hardly cared what happened. Yet more than anything else she dreaded inactivity and the chance it gave her to brood. It was for this reason more than any other that she attempted the rash feat of swimming the mile of water at the river's mouth separating her from the far shore, and consequently from the outer world. She had bid good-bye to her friends, put most of her clothing and her share of the provisions in a small pack tied upon her head, slipped into the water, and struck out. For some time she had swum strongly, but before she had approached the other shore she was tiring rapidly. The slow current was carrying her toward the sea, round a great bend in the river. At last when she looked back she could no longer see the women on the bank far behind her. Then, just before exhaustion overtook her, a native canoe had slipped from the willows and a lithe black paddler had lifted her to safety.

The native was a young chief. He had come to fish in the estuary, and had sat all the afternoon among the willows catching catfish. He had caught all that he wanted, and was preparing to make the trip back up the river to his kraal. Suddenly, to his great amazement, he had seen a very beautiful girl, whose skin was apparently white—white as white mimosa blossoms—swimming feebly, and being carried seaward. He had shot out with his canoe and lifted her into it.

She had gone with him to his kraal; nothing was of great importance now. She had liked the fertile country and the worship she received from the young chief and his natives. At last she had given him her body and her hand in native marriage. And she had not been unhappy in her long lifetime apart from her own people. Several times she had met others of the women who had survived the wreck. They all had native husbands, but their stories were not of violence. As lotus-eaters, they forgot their native land, and were happy here.

The woman before us smiled as if to say 'There is little more to tell.' And then she asked us a little proudly, 'I am white, am I not, to come of a strain into which dark blood had been twice intermixed? I am really lighter than my mother.'

We assured her that she was as white as any English lady, and I added 'much more interesting.' She invited us to stay to dinner, but as we thought it necessary to return to Kow Kenny as soon as possible we declined with thanks. As we rode homeward my mind was filled with the story of the wreck, and I wondered greatly that even in such an early day the natives were maligned to the outer world.

CHINUA ACHEBE

NIGERIA

The Ancestors Judge A Lawsuit

From *Things Fall Apart*. The ancestors or *egwugwu* are the masked elders of the village who perform here the role of judges in a civil dispute. The case has been brought by Uzowulu, who claims that his wife, Mgbafo, has deserted him, and she in turn accuses him of persistently ill-treating her. This short extract from *Things Fall Apart* gives expression to one of the central themes of the novel and of Ibo society, the relationship between traditional authority and the free individual.

At first you may have the impression that these villagers have a superstitious fear of the masked figures, but soon it is clear that they know the man beneath the mask. The running from the masks is more like a ritualized expression of respect than real fear—'they all fled in terror, only to return to their places almost immediately'. The masks are the representatives of the traditional authority and wisdom of the past which is the gift of the ancestors to the living members of the tribe. Even the judges are subject to this law, which depends not on the power of any one man, or even any group, but on the whole society's acceptance of its values. So you will notice how all of the people here are involved in the case, observing the law in action, responding to it with a shout of derision or a murmur of approval. When the titled men put on their masks, it is not dictatorial powers they take on, but a responsibility for preserving the shared values of the community. The observant, critical individual is watching every event here, and from time to time you will hear his voice, establishing a subtle balance with the authority of the *egwugwu*.

Aru oyim de de de dei! flew around the dark, closed hut like tongues of fire. The ancestral spirits of the clan were abroad. The metal gong beat continuously now and the flute, shrill and powerful, floated on the chaos.

And then the *egwugwu* appeared. The women and children sent up a great shout and took to their heels. It was instinctive. A woman fled as soon as an *egwugwu* came in sight. And when, as on that day, nine of the greatest masked spirits in the clan came out together it was a terrifying spectacle. Even Mgbafo took to her heels and had to be restrained by her brothers.

Each of the nine *egwugwu* represented a village of the clan. Their leader was called Evil Forest. Smoke poured out of his head.

The nine villages of Umuofia had grown out of the nine sons of the first father of the clan. Evil Forest represented the village of Umueru, or the children of Eru, who was the eldest of the nine sons.

'*Umuofia kwenu!*' shouted the leading *egwugwu*, pushing the air with his raffia arms. The elders of the clan replied, '*Yaa!*'

'*Umuofia kwenu!*'

'*Yaa!*'

'*Umuofia kwenu!*'

'*Yaa!*'

Evil Forest then thrust the pointed end of his rattling staff into the earth. And it began to shake and rattle, like something agitating with a metallic life. He took the first of the empty stools and the eight other *egwugwu* began to sit in order of seniority after him.

Okonkwo's wives, and perhaps other women as well, might have noticed that the second *egwugwu* had the springy walk of Okonkwo. And they might also have noticed that Okonkwo was not among the titled men and elders who sat behind the row of *egwugwu*. But if they thought these things they kept them within themselves. The *egwugwu* with the springy walk was one of the dead fathers of the clan. He looked terrible with the smoked raffia body, a huge wooden face painted white except for the round hollow eyes and the charred teeth that were as big as a man's fingers. On his head were two powerful horns.

When all the *egwugwu* had sat down and the sound of the many tiny bells and rattles on their bodies had subsided, Evil Forest addressed the two groups of people facing them.

'Uzowulu's body, I salute you,' he said. Spirits always addressed humans as 'bodies'. Uzowulu bent down and touched the earth with his right hand as a sign of submission.

'Our father, my hand has touched the ground,' he said.

'Uzowulu's body, do you know me?' asked the spirit.

'How can I know you, father? You are beyond our knowledge.'

Evil Forest then turned to the other group and addressed the eldest of the three brothers.

'The body of Odukwe, I greet you,' he said, and Odukwe bent down and touched the earth. The hearing then began.

Uzowulu stepped forward and presented his case.

'That woman standing there is my wife, Mgbafo. I married her with my money and my yams. I do not owe my in-laws anything. I owe them no yams. I owe them no cocoyams. One morning three of them came to my house, beat me up and took my wife and children away. This happened in the rainy season. I have waited in vain for my wife to return. At last I went to my in-laws and said to them, "You have taken back your sister. I did not send her away. You yourselves took her. The law of the clan is that you should return her bride-price." But my wife's brothers said they had nothing to tell me. So I have brought the matter to the fathers of the clan. My case is finished. I salute you.'

'Your words are good,' said the leader of the *egwugwu*. 'Let us hear Odukwe. His words may also be good.'

Odukwe was short and thick-set. He stepped forward, saluted the spirits and began his story.

'My in-law has told you that we went to his house, beat him up and took our sister and her children away. All that is true. He told you that he came to take back her bride-price and we refused to give it him. That also is true. My in-law, Uzowulu, is a beast. My sister lived with him for nine years. During those years no single day passed in the sky without his beating

the woman. We have tried to settle their quarrels time without
number and on each occasion Uzowulu was guilty—'

'It is a lie!' Uzowulu shouted.

'Two years ago,' continued Odukwe, 'when she was pregnant, he beat her until she miscarried.'

'It is a lie. She miscarried after she had gone to sleep with
her lover.'

'Uzowulu's body, I salute you,' said Evil Forest, silencing
him. 'What kind of lover sleeps with a pregnant woman?'
There was a loud murmur of approbation from the crowd.
Odukwe continued:

'Last year when my sister was recovering from an illness,
he beat her again so that if the neighbours had not gone in to
save her she would have been killed. We heard of it, and did
as you have been told. The law of Umuofia is that if a woman
runs away from her husband her bride-price is returned. But
in this case she ran away to save her life. Her two children
belong to Uzowulu. We do not dispute it, but they are too
young to leave their mother. If, on the other hand, Uzowulu
should recover from his madness and come in the proper way to
beg his wife to return she will do so on the understanding that
if he ever beats her again we shall cut off his genitals for him.'

The crowd roared with laughter. Evil Forest rose to his feet
and order was immediately restored. A steady cloud of smoke
rose from his head. He sat down again and called two witnesses.
They were both Uzowulu's neighbours, and they agreed about
the beating. Evil Forest then stood up, pulled out his staff and
thrust it into the earth again. He ran a few steps in the direction
of the women; they all fled in terror, only to return to their
places almost immediately. The nine *egwugwu* then went away
to consult together in their house. They were silent for a long
time. Then the metal gong sounded and the flute was blown.
The *egwugwu* had emerged once again from their underground
home. They saluted one another and then reappeared on the *ilo*.

'*Umuofia kwenu!*' roared Evil Forest, facing the elders and grandees of the clan.

'*Yaa!*' replied the thunderous crowd; then silence descended from the sky and swallowed the noise.

Evil Forest began to speak and all the while he spoke everyone was silent. The eight other *egwugwu* were as still as statues.

'We have heard both sides of the case,' said Evil Forest. 'Our duty is not to blame this man or to praise that, but to settle the dispute.' He turned to Uzowulu's group and allowed a short pause.

'Uzowulu's body, do you know me?'

'How can I know you, father? You are beyond our knowledge,' Uzowulu replied.

'I am Evil Forest. I kill a man on the day that his life is sweetest to him.'

'That is true,' replied Uzowulu.

'Go to your in-laws with a pot of wine and beg your wife to return to you. It is not bravery when a man fights with a woman.' He turned to Odukwe, and allowed a brief pause.

'Odukwe's body, I greet you,' he said.

'My hand is on the ground,' replied Odukwe.

'Do you know me?'

'No man can know you,' replied Odukwe.

'I am Evil Forest, I am Dry-meat-that-fills-the-mouth, I am Fire-that-burns-without-faggots. If your in-law brings wine to you, let your sister go with him. I salute you.' He pulled his staff from the hard earth and thrust it back.

'*Umuofia kwenu!*' he roared, and the crowd answered.

'I don't know why such a trifle should come before the *egwugwu*,' said one elder to another.

'Don't you know what kind of man Uzowulu is? He will not listen to any other decision,' replied the other.

As they spoke two other groups of people had replaced the first before the *egwugwu*, and a great land case began.

SOLOMON ATTOH AHUMA

GHANA

Black Whitemen

From *The Gold Coast Nation and National Consciousness*. Solomon
Attoh Ahuma, along with such men as J. E. Casley-Hayford and
J. Mensah Sarbah, must be considered among the fathers of Ghana's
independence. He was constantly active in politics, education and
journalism from the end of the nineteenth century until his death
in 1922. But in this extract from one of his essays, you may recognize
the kind of strain which must have been felt by many West Africans
of this period and since. On one hand there was their nationalism,
their need for independence, but on the other there was their British
education and their attachments to British values—for almost all
the political leaders of this period were lawyers or clergymen.

So as you read this extract I think you will become aware of a
conflict in the author's mind, reflected in the way he writes. While
he denounces the young West African who tries to be a 'Whiteman',
Attoh Ahuma himself uses the language and style of the nineteenth-
century English essay, he quotes approvingly from patriotic English
verse, and he ends by proposing, almost as the summit of African
achievement, 'the respect and admiration of the Whiteman.'

You may feel that this weakens his argument. But there is a further
possibility which I would like you to consider. Do you recognize
any irony in some of his praise of 'Whitemen' and their institutions;
isn't the remark about their being very 'clubbable' a bit double-
edged? This strikes me as the kind of praise which sometimes makes
the recipient slightly uncomfortable, and one might wonder exactly
how seriously it was intended.

The Churchill mentioned here, incidentally, is not Sir Winston
but Charles, an eighteenth-century poet.

Imitation, it is said, is the sincerest form of flattery; but,
according to Jonathan Swift in his *Cadenus and Vanessa*,
'FLATTERY'S THE FOOD OF FOOLS'. Histrionism is undoubtedly
the special *forte* of the educated West African; he is a copyist
to the pitch of profane excellence. The Whiteman has his
vices as well as his virtues, and sometimes the vices of his

virtues. To follow him half-way therefore, is not, and cannot
be the sincerest form of flattery. The average West African
of the Molluscan Order is a clever imitator of everything the
Whiteman thinks, and does, and says, particularly in the out-
ward appearance and observance. If he doffed his coat and
went about in his shirt sleeves in broad daylight, by reason of
our intolerable tropical heat, his Native understudy faithfully
followed suit; if, in the cool of the evening, he discarded his
headgear, the backboneless myrmidons did likewise. As he
lands in the latest things in vogue, his echo takes full notes,
and, in less than seven weeks, like a puppet or marionette he
sports the identical style and fashion. Thanks to the letters
C.O.D., facilities are afforded the young upstart to gratify his
unworthy ambition. What the Whiteman eats, he eats; what
he drinks and smokes, he drinks and smokes, thereby securing
what, in his deluded opinion, is considered the Hall-mark of
respectability, civilization and refinement. If his lord and
master holds a cigar in a peculiar manner, it is copied; his gait,
mode of expression, his expletives, smiles, laughter and other
mannerisms and peculiarities, are all taken in wholesale, and
reproduced with the fidelity of an Edisonian Phonograph.
These are the things the black wretch, in his Bœotian ignorance
and folly, regards as signs of perfect manhood—this thin
veneer of polish—and there the lesson ends. The thoughtful,
judicious and discreet Young African, naturally versed in the
principles of Selection—who differentiates and discriminates
between essentials and unessentials, who studiously rejects
and selects, skips what does not concern him or does not
correspond with its environments, who recognizes limitations,
and is independent of foreign ways, customs and manners, is
accordingly ridiculed and reprobated as *de trop* and unclassed.
He is a Hottentot or a Bushman who does not successfully
compete with the Whiteman in his sartorial equipment.

These unthinking young men and women are some of the

problems of the country. It is no standard of excellence for a common clerk earning £50 per annum to rival and beat into a cock-hat his employer or superior officer drawing £500 a year, plus a Duty Allowance three times as much as is allowed to the native assistant. It is time enough for such monstrosities to learn that *The Mind is the standard of the man* and that *Righteousness exalteth a nation.* The European with his lucrative position and rich emoluments is never a Walking Drapery. He fully knows the limit of things, and acts upon fixed principles—he is not a slave to the whims, fancies and caprice of passing fashion-vogue or the luxuries and dainties of the larder and the cellar. He has been taught from his youth how to draw the line and say, HITHER, BUT NO FURTHER; he has sufficient backbone to pull up when necessary—at any rate, such are the qualities that the majority of Whitemen consider the true indications of healthy and progressive manhood. If, therefore, by reason of our irregular, imperfect and extraneous training, we must learn from them, it is absolutely necessary, for our own good and in the higher interests of our Country, Nation and Race, that we imitate them in those excellencies that make for genuine progress and advancement. The Whiteman is essentially a clubbable fellow; he is naturally gregarious, and has, in his mental and moral equipment, those graces and virtues which help to cement Friendship, promote Unity, and bring about successful issues in all undertakings. He knows when, where and how to defend his countryman; he has been fed with the sincere milk of co-operation and combination. And as Churchill has taught him, he could always say with unction and pride of Race and Country:

> Be England what she will,
> With all her faults She is my Country still:

Or Cowper:—

> England, with all thy faults I love thee still,
> My Country.

And in the same proportion and with equal sincerity, he extends the right hand of fellowship and *camaraderie* to his compatriot wherever, and in what circumstances soever found. He stands shoulder to shoulder with him in weal or woe, by good report or ill, and in the bond of perfect amity. In these notable respects, the Englishman is worthy of imitation. It is never to the credit of any West African to strive manfully to become Anglo-African, Europeanized or Anglicized in anything. A Black Whiteman is a creature, a freak, and a monstrosity.

To be so civilized as to be ashamed of one's own Name, and Country and Nation, and all that these principal factors connote, is to betray the possession of principles and things that in Pandemonium are worshipped, adored, and glorified. It is no criterion of progress—it is the embodiment of retrogression—to copy the cut of the Whiteman's coat without making one's own [the] other interests he boasts of. He despises in his heart of hearts all extravagance, thoughtlessness and stupidity. He laughs with his native counterpart and pats him on the back calling him a *jolly good fellow*; but he enjoys his private opinion of all his monkey trickeries and clever performances. Many have gone too far and must pull up so that by living within their means, by revising their judgment in most matters European, and by copying the bright examples that stud the pages of British History, we may all wake up to the glorious possibilities of our Country and take entire possession of our grand inheritance. With increased knowledge of all kinds, social, intellectual and moral, side by side with increased responsibilities—and using all our acquisitions for the good of the Race accordingly—recognizing and realizing those responsibilities, so will West Africa be proportionately civilized and prospered—so may we command the respect and admiration of the Whiteman.

PETER ABRAHAMS

SOUTH AFRICA

The Young Bosses

This extract comes from Peter Abrahams' autobiography, *Tell Freedom*, about growing up in South Africa. Here he learns what happens to a coloured boy who tries to fight back. You'll notice that both his friend, Andries and his uncle, Sam, solve the problem by giving way—Andries runs for cover when the white boys chase him, Sam beats Lee (i.e. Peter) when the white man orders him to. Do you think that, in their situation, they could do anything else? And when Andries says to Lee 'God, you're dumb. You're going to get it,' what do you think about his attitude? Is it sensible?

When this episode begins, Lee and Andries see a group of white schoolboys coming towards them.

There were three of them. Two of about our own size and one slightly bigger. They had school bags and were coming toward us up the road from the siding.

'Better run for it,' Andries said.

'Why?'

'No, that'll draw them. Let's just walk along, but quickly.'

'Why?' I repeated.

'Shut up,' he said.

Some of his anxiety touched me. Our own scrap was forgotten. We marched side by side as fast as we could. The white boys saw us and hurried up the road. We passed the fork. Perhaps they would take the turning away from us. We dared not look back.

'Hear them?' Andries asked.

'No.'

I looked over my shoulder.

'They're coming,' I said.

'Walk faster,' Andries said. 'If they come closer, run.'

'Hey, *klipkop*!'

26

'Don't look back,' Andries said.

'Hottentot!'

We walked as fast as we could.

'Bloody kaffir!'

Ahead was a bend in the road. Behind the bend were bushes. Once there, we could run without them knowing it till it was too late.

'Faster,' Andries said.

They began pelting us with stones.

'Run when we get to the bushes,' Andries said.

The bend and the bushes were near. We would soon be there.

A clear young voice carried to us:

'Your fathers are dirty black bastards of baboons!'

'Run!' Andries called.

A violent, unreasoning anger suddenly possessed me. I stopped and turned.

'You're a liar!' I screamed it.

The foremost boy pointed at me:

'An ugly black baboon!'

In a fog of rage I went towards him.

'Liar!' I shouted. 'My father was better than your father!'

I neared them. The bigger boy stepped between me and the one I was after.

'My father was better than your father! Liar!'

The big boy struck me a mighty clout on the side of the face. I staggered, righted myself, and leapt at the boy who had insulted my father. I struck him on the face hard. A heavy blow on the back of my head nearly stunned me. I grabbed at the boy in front of me. We went down together.

'Liar!' I said through clenched teeth, hitting him with all my might.

Blows rained on me, on my head, my neck, the side of my face, my mouth, but my enemy was under me and I pounded him fiercely, all the time repeating:

'Liar! Liar! Liar!'

Suddenly, stars exploded in my head. Then there was darkness.

I emerged from darkness to find Andries kneeling beside me.

'God man! I thought they'd killed you.'

I sat up. The white boys were nowhere to be seen. Like Andries, they'd probably thought me dead and run off in panic. The inside of my mouth felt sore and swollen. My nose was tender to the touch. The back of my head ached. A trickle of blood dripped from my nose. I stemmed it with the square of coloured cloth. Greatest damage was to my shirt. It was ripped in many places. I remembered the crackling. I looked anxiously about. It was safe, a little off the road on the grass. I relaxed. I got up and brushed my clothes. I picked up the crackling.

'God, you're dumb!' Andries said. 'You're going to get it! Dumb arse!'

I was too depressed to retort. Besides, I knew he was right. I was dumb. I should have run when he told me to.

'Come on,' I said.

One of many small groups of children, each child carrying his little bag of crackling, we trod the long road home in the cold winter afternoon.

There was tension in the house that night. When I got back Aunt Liza had listened to the story in silence. The beating or scolding I expected did not come. But Aunt Liza changed while she listened, became remote and withdrawn. When Uncle Sam came home she told him what had happened. He, too, just looked at me and became more remote and withdrawn than usual. They were waiting for something; their tension reached out to me, and I waited with them, anxious, apprehensive.

The thing we waited for came while we were having our supper. We heard a trap pull up outside.

'Here it is,' Uncle Sam said and got up.

Aunt Liza leaned back from the table and put her hands in her lap, fingers intertwined, a cold, unseeing look in her eyes.

Before Uncle Sam reached it, the door burst open. A tall, broad, white man strode in. Behind him came the three boys. The one I had attacked had swollen lips and a puffy left eye.

'Evening *baas*,' Uncle Sam murmured.

'That's him,' the bigger boy said, pointing at me.

The white man stared till I lowered my eyes.

'Well?' he said.

'He's sorry, *baas*,' Uncle Sam said quickly. 'I've given him a hiding he won't forget soon. You know how it is, *baas*. He's new here, the child of a relative in Johannesburg and they don't all know how to behave there. You know how it is in the big towns, *baas*.' The plea in Uncle Sam's voice had grown more pronounced as he went on. He turned to me. 'Tell the *baas* and young *basies* how sorry you are, Lee.'

I looked at Aunt Liza and something in her lifelessness made me stubborn in spite of my fear.

'He insulted my father,' I said.

The white man smiled.

'See Sam, your hiding couldn't have been good.'

There was a flicker of life in Aunt Liza's eyes. For a brief moment she saw me, looked at me, warmly, lovingly, then her eyes went dead again.

'He's only a child, *baas*,' Uncle Sam murmured.

'You stubborn too, Sam?'

'No, *baas*.'

'Good...Then teach him, Sam. If you and he are to live here, you must teach him. Well...?'

'Yes, *baas*.'

Uncle Sam went into the other room and returned with a thick leather thong. He wound it once round his hand and advanced on me. The man and boys leaned against the door, watching. I looked at Aunt Liza's face. Though there was no sign of life or feeling on it, I knew suddenly, instinctively, that she wanted me not to cry.

Bitterly, Uncle Sam said:

'You must never lift your hand to a white person. No matter what happens, you must never lift your hand to a white person...'

He lifted the strap and brought it down on my back. I clenched my teeth and stared at Aunt Liza. I did not cry with the first three strokes. Then, suddenly, Aunt Liza went limp. Tears showed in her eyes. The thong came down on my back, again and again. I screamed and begged for mercy. I grovelled at Uncle Sam's feet, begging him to stop, promising never to lift my hand to any white person...

At last, the white man's voice said:

'All right, Sam.'

Uncle Sam stopped. I lay whimpering on the floor. Aunt Liza sat like one in a trance.

'Is he still stubborn, Sam?'

'Tell the *baas* and *basies* you are sorry.'

'I'm sorry,' I said.

'Bet his father is one of those who believe in equality.'

'His father is dead,' Aunt Liza said.

'Good night, Sam.'

'Good night, *baas*. Sorry about this.'

'All right, Sam.' He opened the door. The boys went out first, then he followed. 'Good night, Liza.'

Aunt Liza did not answer. The door shut behind the white folk, and, soon, we heard their trap moving away. Uncle Sam flung the thong viciously against the door, slumped down on the bench, folded his arms on the table, and buried his head in his arms. Aunt Liza moved away from him, came on the floor beside me and lifted me into her large lap. She sat rocking my body. Uncle Sam began to sob softly. After some time, he raised his head and looked at us.

'Explain to the child, Liza,' he said.

'You explain,' Aunt Liza said bitterly. 'You are the man. You did the beating. You are the head of the family. This is a man's world. You do the explaining.'

'Please, Liza...'

'You should be happy. The whites are satisfied. We can go on now.'

With me in her arms, Aunt Liza got up. She carried me into the other room. The food on the table remained half-eaten. She laid me on the bed on my stomach, smeared fat on my back, then covered me with blankets. She undressed and got into bed beside me. She cuddled me close, warmed me with her own body. With her big hand on my cheek, she rocked me, first to silence, then to sleep.

WILLIAM PLOMER
SOUTH AFRICA

Ula Masondo and Friends

From *Ula Masondo*. The hero of William Plomer's story is an innocent country boy come to town, rather like Sylvester Stein's Staffnurse Phopholo whom you may remember from the first volume. The people in the town don't have much time for him, and so it isn't very surprising that when a group of minor criminals make him feel at home he gladly joins them. Here, Vilakazi, the leader, and his gang are about to plan a burglary.

In spare time Vilakazi and Ula Masondo now had the company of Stefan, the *leita* man-of-the-world, and also that of Emma, now unattached to her white man, lately convicted of forgery. She took to coming with a friend, called Smile by Europeans, and by his own people Isimayili.

It became the custom of these five to meet in a thicket of steevrugte bushes on an unfrequented part of the kopje near the mine. Here, unseen by the rest of the world, they had a view of the road below them in the valley, and beyond, among the hills, a prospect of the roofs and dumps of the inner suburbs of Goldenville.

Ula Masondo, youngest and most ingenuous of the five, now lived in a constant excitement, almost willingly giving up his money to buy drink, cigarettes, and the goodwill of his elders, and quite willingly giving up all his attention to their talk. He had never felt so important, and was trying at one time to flatter the giant Vilakazi, to imitate Stefan, and to make an impression on Emma, when he was completely distracted by the novelty of Smile.

Smile, short and powerful, never stopped smiling when sober, but when drunk he tried to bite. He had already at different times bitten a horse, a postman, and a missionary, and when, on one occasion, he suddenly fastened his teeth in the arm of Emma, she uttered shriek after shriek as if her soul was leaving her body, and attracted the attention of a native policeman, who blew his whistle so near at hand, so un-expectedly, that Smile, drunk as he was, at once withdrew his incisive caress. The five of them lay flat on their bellies under the bushes, and Emma put her fist in her mouth to stop herself screaming, and nearly choked in consequence with pain, hysterics, and anxiety. They could hear the policeman panting past them on his way up the hill. He stumbled, rummaging among the rocks, and even stopped to beat the tops of the very bushes in which the party lay breathlessly hidden. When it was safe to speak again, Smile had begun to snore in a drunken stupor, and Emma was nursing her bleeding arm. The tears gushed down her face, and in future, as soon as Smile began to drink, she always sat as far away from him as possible, in order to avoid his sadistic attentions.

To his masters Smile appeared simply as a cheerful house-boy. He worked in a respectable slum for two small semi-detached houses that shared one kitchen. One of his masters was a solitary old bachelor, a retired sergeant-major with waxed moustaches. The other was a Flemish-South African carpenter who had formerly been in the Congo (O Cosmopolis!), and was so tolerant of Smile that he was ready to treat him almost as one of the family, but his wife, a Danish-Swiss, a lazy woman with a grudge against life, treated her husband like a child, her children like servants, and Smile like a dog. When she gave him his wages she used to say bitterly:

'Here's your bone, *chien fidèle*. Now go and bury it.'

After which she would clout him with a frying-pan and go back to bed.

On Sunday mornings Smile wore a black coat, and carried in his pocket a Lambu Bible, for he belonged to one of those innumerable native sects that make of Christianity an exciting cult, and quote the Scriptures to their own purposes. In the afternoons he still had the Bible with him, and used also to carry a little cane, which he would wave like a wand, saying of somebody he disliked, in a tone of the utmost contempt:

'Hau! He's just a heathen!'

or describing something he liked:

'Truly, this tobacco is Christian!'

There was in his character a considerable strength. With little persuasion Emma would have allowed him to chew her into rags. As for Ula Masondo, he even got the permission of Vilakazi to buy a little cane, which he began to wave adroitly in imitation of Smile.

As for Ula Masondo, fascinated by the daring and sinister insouciance of Stefan, obsessed with the Christian dandyism of Smile, and infatuated with the over-ripe charms of Emma, he began to feel more independent than usual of Vilakazi, his first patron and worldly guide. He and Vilakazi were, in fact, heading for a quarrel, when, in reviewing their debts, they found that some must be paid. Money they must have. While financial adversity kept them together, Smile, with a barbaric and original smile in which there was more naïveté than cunning, unexpectedly hinted at a sum that he supposed to be not less than £50.

It appeared that the carpenter and his family had decided to spend the next week-end visiting friends in the country, and Smile had already been told that he would be expected to guard the house.

'As if I was a watch-dog,' he explained. But if only his other, ex-military master could be temporarily transferred from one house to the other, the money would be theirs.

Vilakazi had lately been thinking more of getting Emma than of getting money, but now he sat up, stretched his arms, and began to take notice.

'What money?' Stefan was asking with an air of tired dignity.

'The money we want!' said Smile, smiling.

'Where is it, this money of yours?'

'You say it's mine? The money of Shortlegs!'

'Who is Shortlegs?'

'My baas!'

'One of your baases, you mean. Where does he hide this money?'

'Under his bed.'

'Shades of my fathers! How do you know?'

'I've seen him.'

'What did you see?'

'I saw him put money in a box under his bed.'

'How much?'

'A lot! Pounds and pounds!'

'Fifty pounds?'

'Do I know?'
'Where were you, then?'
'Looking through the window.'
'Is it a big box?'
'No, small. So big.'
'Is Shortlegs married?'
'No.'
'Has he got a girl?'
'Do I know? Sometimes he goes out at nights. Do I know where he goes?'
'It is plain what we must do.'
'How, then?'
'Early on Sunday afternoon you, Isimayili, will be sitting in your outhouse talking to Emma. Then you will go and make a big fire of papers and sticks on the back *stoep* of the carpenter's house, and start shouting: "Fire! Fire!" Emma will run through the kitchen and call to Shortlegs that the house is on fire. He will see that she is a fine girl and will come running with her to see what is the matter—'
'No!' said Emma vigorously, 'I don't want that!'
'What do you want, then? It is your work, I say, to bring Shortlegs out of his house.'
'I don't want! I don't want!'
'Shut up!' said Stefan. 'When Emma and Shortlegs come through the kitchen you, Isimayili, will be shouting and beating out the fire—make as much smoke as you can!—then Vilakazi will run into the kitchen to stop Shortlegs if he tries to come back. Meanwhile, I will run in for the box, and I'll throw it over the wall to you, Masondo, who will catch it on the other side. Then you must run. I shall run just after you, and Vilakazi must run after me. But each of us three must run a different way, and we will meet here afterwards. You, Isimayili, will stay in your outhouse with Emma and say you know nothing about anything.'

Ula Masondo was amazed at the ingenuity of this plan.

When the time came, after many preliminary thrills, Ula Masondo heard a crackle of sticks and Smile's voice crying 'Fire!' and peeped over the wall just in time to see Emma leaping out of the back door with a jingle of jewellery, followed immediately by the ex-soldier, who had just been to sleep. With a scarlet face and moustaches like hat-pins, this veteran was trying to make haste slowly like an officer and a gentleman, though his beery eyes were goggling with panic. As soon as he had dashed into the kitchen, Vilakazi followed, and Stefan sprang out from behind a water-tank and darted into the house.

There was at once a smell of smoke and sounds could be heard of excited voices, pattering feet, and water hissing and sizzling.

Back came Stefan, hurdling over the wall, with the box under his arm. He threw it to Ula Masondo, and hearing a scuffle in the kitchen they both made off as fast as they could.

They were already crouching in the bushes, and trying to force open the box, when Vilakazi arrived panting and drenched with sweat.

'How was it, Vilakazi?'

'Hau! Isimayili put out the fire too quickly, and Shortlegs came back too soon. He isn't Shortlegs, he is Satane. He kicked like the devil and screamed like a pig. Can a person hold a screaming pig with a devil inside? There you are, I threw him under the table, and there you are, I have come!'

He wiped the sweat from his face with a handkerchief of magenta silk, and then lay down on his back to recover his wind, but, Stefan succeeding at that moment in bursting open the lid of the box, he at once sat up again. The money only amounted to £23, and the three spent the rest of the afternoon in the frantic exhilaration of deciding how it was to be divided.

JOHN E. OCANSEY

GHANA

Encounters with English Children

From *African Trading; or The Trials of William Narh Ocansey.* This book was written by John Ocansey, the son of a merchant of Addah on the River Volta, after a visit to England on business in 1880. He reveals in his book a very pleasing gentleness of manner, particularly in those passages describing the children he saw, whose life and behaviour he appeared to enjoy observing.

On Sunday the 26th of June, I visited the Blue-coat School where many young orphan boys and girls are taken in and educated. After passing through and inspecting the apartments in which they live, I went into their church to attend the service. It was a large building capable of holding 2,000 persons, besides all the Blue-coat scholars, which number about 300, and 100 lady teachers, singers and servants. The Church was very full, and I was told that the people come to hear the singing which is very fine, for the scholars are well trained. After the people were all seated, the organist came in and began to play a soft sweet exercise, which I thought to be part of the service. The pulpit was there, but there was no one in it, and I began to feel uneasy about the minister—why did he delay? had he not arrived? was he taken ill? Still the organist went on playing what appeared a long time. But see! now he pulls out the stops of the organ and rises to his exercise with great energy and changes the sound of the organ until it is like a large band of music marching. I could hardly think it was the organ, for I thought I heard many instruments, and the drums beating, and it swelled louder and louder in great deep tones until the place shook with the sound. Then he played a fine march and the scholars, boys and girls, came marching in, two by two, so close that they touched each other in walking, and kept step to the music most correctly. Oh, how nice and pleasant it was, and how clean and healthy they all appeared! Nothing pleased me more than the large white broad collars over their necks. They came marching on through the middle of the Church with steady, solid step to the tones of the drum-playing organ. Then one little boy, about ten years of age, ascended into the pulpit, and taking the hymn-book, gave out the hymn like an aged minister. Then the organist, after preparing his stops, began to play, and all the people rise and sing:—

> Before Jehovah's awful throne
> Ye nations bow with sacred joy;
> Know that the Lord is God alone,
> He can create and He destroy.

After that twelve boys came forward in a line just before the organ and pulpit, and one of them, taking a book called a Catechism, asked the others a great many questions which they answered very willingly, and with great ability. Then six girls came forward, and they were asked many questions out of the Bible, and they also answered very correctly and cleverly. A collection was then made, and afterwards a hymn sung, and the little boy gave the benediction. Then without the least noise or confusion, they form into procession, and march out to the sound of the organ. We followed them, and passed through their eating rooms. Their evening meal was then prepared and on the tables; their bread on wooden plates and their tea and milk in tin cups. I was told that they were all poor and destitute children that were taken in, who had no father or mother, and that the expense of keeping them is defrayed by some of the people of the city, who give yearly subscriptions, as they think fit.

As I passed along the streets, I noticed the people looking at me very earnestly. The small boys especially would stand

and stare, and would sometimes call out to me, 'Halloa! blacky, can't you wash your face before you come out in the morning and make it white?' My companion kindly said, 'You must not take any notice of them, because they do not know any better.'

A few days after I had been in Liverpool, and was walking down the streets, a small boy ran up to me, and touched his cap to salute me. I thought, perhaps he knew me. He then pointed down to my boots, and I looked down too, for I began to be uneasy, thinking there was something wrong with my feet; but the boy continued touching his cap and pointing to my boots, and crying out 'Shine, sir!' 'Shine, sir, only a penny!' Then I saw he had blacking and brushes, and a little stand to rest the foot on; and he wanted to earn a penny by blackening my boots.

In the afternoon and evenings especially, quite a large number of small boys and girls are in the streets selling newspapers. And they are very quick and watch every person, going up or down the street to see if they will buy one. Now I like the newspaper. It is a luxury to me as it is to the white man. It is very cheap; and contains much information from all parts, and about many things. Then I thought I would buy one, and I put my hand in my pocket to see if I had a copper. Instantly the boys and girls detected my intention, and half-a-dozen came bounding towards me and, thrusting their papers at me, said 'Please buy from me!' 'Please take mine; I saw you first!' and I could hardly get away from them.

My friends in Liverpool are very kind to me, and often ask me to their private houses. I went with one friend, and he introduced me to his family, one little boy and two girls. During the evening, one of the little girls, about six years of age, came and said to me, 'Mr Ocansey, I wish when you go back to Africa that you would send your little black boy here, and then he could carry my books to school for me.' The father said, 'Mary, my love, what are you saying? Suppose I give you to Mr Ocansey, and he will take you to Africa, and then you will have to carry the books for the black boy?' She looked round smart, and said, 'But I shall not go to Africa, the sun will make me a black girl, and you said just now that they have no good schools in Africa.'

On another occasion, as I was going with a friend to his home, we had to go down a street leading to the docks, when a poor white boy came and ran along with us, begging for a penny. He looked so beseechingly, and begged so strongly, that I said to him, 'What is it you want?' He said, 'A penny, please!' And I was just going to give him one, when my friend said, 'No! do not do it; you encourage begging, and we want to put it down; for no one in England need beg in the street if they are honest and willing to work.' But the boy still followed us, and he looked so miserable that I gave him a penny...

NUPE FOLK TALE

NIGERIA

The Talking Skull

From *African Genesis*. This neat and simple tale doesn't, as you'll see, have a moral at the end. Do you think it needs one? And if it did have a moral at the end, would there be any point in telling the story?

A hunter goes into the bush. He finds an old human skull. The hunter says: 'What brought you here?' The skull answers: 'Talking brought me here.' The hunter runs off. He runs to the king. He tells the king: 'I found a dry human skull in the bush. It asks you how its father and mother are.'

The king says: 'Never since my mother bore me have I heard that a dead skull can speak.' The king summons the Alkali, the Saba, and the Degi and asks them if they have ever heard the like. None of the wise men has heard the like and they decide to send a guard out with the hunter into the bush to find out if his story is true and, if so, to learn the reason for it. The guard accompany the hunter into the bush with the order to kill him on the spot should he have lied. The guard and the hunter come to the skull. The hunter addresses the skull: 'Skull, speak.' The skull is silent. The hunter asks as before: 'What brought you here?' The skull does not answer. The whole day long the hunter begs the skull to speak, but it does not answer. In the evening the guard tell the hunter to make the skull speak, and when he cannot they kill him in accordance with the king's command. When the guard are gone the skull opens its jaws and asks the dead hunter's head: 'What brought you here?' The dead hunter's head replies: 'Talking brought me here!'

JAMES NGUGI

KENYA

The Road Across the Land

From *Weep Not, Child*. This is a novel about the rise of Mau Mau, and these early pages from it describe some of the conflicts underlying the rebellion. The person speaking here is not the author, but a character created by him—an imaginary Kenyan who is thinking about the society he lives in. He is a puzzled man, for he asks himself question after question—'Who made the road?', 'Why should the white man have fought?', 'Was the Indian a white man?', 'Did he come from England?'—and after each question he tries to offer some kind of answer, not always very successfully. The new road is the big question at the centre of all this—who built it? why

was it built? where does it lead? Apparently it leads to a world
inhabited by white men and Indians and all the problems they
raise, but now that it has been built the African must begin to travel
on it. The road was the result of another puzzle, the war in which
the white men fought their own brothers, in which the invincible
English were seen, for the first time, to be vulnerable and to have
fears and problems of their own—'Ah, Hitler, that brave man, whom
all the British feared...' With the war, the cracks in society have
begun to widen and down the road and into the town come the
young men. The old order is breaking, and in the gangs the boys
call themselves 'young Hitlers'. After you have read this passage,
you might think about why they give themselves this name.

There was only one road that ran right across the land. It was
long and broad and shone with black tar, and when you
travelled along it on hot days you saw little lakes ahead of
you. But when you went near, the lakes vanished, to appear
again a little further ahead. Some people called them the
devil's waters because they deceived you and made you more
thirsty if your throat was already dry. And the road which
ran across the land was long and broad, had no beginning and
no end. At least, few people knew of its origin. Only if you
followed it it would take you to the big city and leave you
there while it went beyond to the unknown, perhaps joining
the sea. Who made the road? Rumour had it that it came with
the white men and some said that it was rebuilt by the Italian
prisoners during the Big War that was fought far away from
here. People did not know how big the war had been because
most of them had never seen a big war fought with planes,
poison, fire and bombs—bombs that would finish a country
just like that when they were dropped from the air. It was
indeed a big war because it made the British worry and pray
and those black sons of the land who had gone to fight said
it was a big war. There was once another big war. The first
one was to drive away the Germans who had threatened to
attack and reduce the black people to slavery. Or so the people
had been told. But that was far away and long ago and only

old men and middle-aged men could remember it. It was not as big as the second because then there were no bombs, and black people did not go to Egypt and Burma.

The Italian prisoners who built the long tarmac road had left a name for themselves because some went about with black women and the black women had white children. Only the children by black mothers and Italian prisoners who were also white men were not really 'white' in the usual way. They were ugly and some grew up to have small wounds all over the body and especially around the mouth so that flies followed them all the time and at all places. Some people said that this was a punishment. Black people should not sleep with white men who ruled them and treated them badly.

Why should the white men have fought? Aaa! You could never tell what these people would do. In spite of the fact that they were all white, they killed one another with poison, fire and big bombs that destroyed the land. They had even called the people to help them in killing one another. It was puzzling. You could not really understand because although they said they fought Hitler (ah! Hitler, that brave man, whom all the British feared, and he was never killed you know, just vanished like that), Hitler too was a white man. That did not take you very far. It was better to give up the attempt and be content with knowing the land you lived in, and the people who lived near you. And if this was not enough and you wanted to see more people and hear stories from far and wide—even stories from across the sea, Russia, England, Burma—you could avoid the vigilance of your wife and go to the local town, Kipanga. You could, for instance, tell her that you were going to buy some meat for the family. That was something...

'All right! Go and don't loiter in the town too much. I know you men. When you want to avoid work you go to the town and drink while we, your slaves, must live in toil and sweat.'

'I'll come back soon.'

'See how you turn your eyes. You cannot even look at me in the face because you know you'll go and stay there the whole day...'

'Now, now, just you trust me to come back soon.'

'The idea of trusting you!'

There were many ways from Mahua village to Kipanga. You could follow the big road. It passed near the town. Or you could follow a track that went through a valley into the town. In a country of ridges, such as Kikuyuland, there are many valleys and small plains. Even the big road went through a valley on the opposite side. Where the two met they had as it were embraced and widened themselves into a plain. The plain, more or less rectangular in shape, had four valleys leading into or out of it at the corners. The first two valleys went into the Country of the Black people. The other two divided the land of the Black People from the land of the White People. This meant that there were four ridges that stood and watched one another. Two of the ridges on the opposite sides of the long sides of the plain were broad and near one another. The other two were narrow and had pointed ends. You could tell the land of Black People because it was red, rough and sickly, while the land of the white settlers was green and was not lacerated into small strips.

Kipanga town was built in this field. It was not a big town like the big city. However, there was one shoe factory and many black people earned their living there. The Indian shops were many. The Indian traders were said to be very rich. They too employed some black boys whom they treated as nothing. You could never like the Indians because their customs were strange and funny in a bad way. But their shops were big and well-stocked with things. White settlers, with their wives and children, often came to the rich Indians and bought all they wanted. The Indians feared Europeans and, if you went to buy in a shop and a white man found you, the Indian would stop selling to you and, trembling all over, would begin to serve him. But some said that this was a cunning way to deceive the white women because when the Indian trembled and was all 'Yes, please, Memsahib, anything more?' the women would be ready to pay any price they were told because they thought an Indian who feared them dared not cheat about prices.

Black people too brought things from the Indians. But they also bought in the African shops which stood alone on one side of the town near the post office. The Africans had not many things in their store and they generally charged higher prices so that although the Indians were not liked and they abused women, using dirty words they had learnt in Swahili, people found it wiser and more convenient to buy from them. Some people said that black people should stick together and take trade only to their black brethren. And one day an old poor woman said, 'Let Africans stick together and charge very low prices. We are all black. If this be not so, then why grudge a poor woman the chance to buy from someone, be he white or red, who charges less money for his things?'

In the Indian bazaar, black people mingled with white people and Indians. You did not know what to call the Indian. Was he also a white man? Did he too come from England? Some people who had been to Burma said that Indians were poor in their country and were too ruled by white men. There was a man in India called Gandhi. This man was a strange prophet. He always fought for the Indian freedom. He was a thin man, and was always dressed poorly in calico stretched over his bony body. Walking along the shops, you could see his photograph in every Indian building. The Indians called him *Babu*, and it was said this Babu was actually their god. He had told them not to go to war so that while black people had been conscripted into the army the Indians had utterly refused and had been left alone. It was rumoured that the white men in Kenya did not like them because they had refused to go to war against Hitler. This showed that the Indians were cowards. The Africans were inclined to agree with this idea of Indian cowardice.

The African shops were built in two rows which faced one another. The air was full of noise and, near the meat shops, there was a strong stench of burning flesh. Some young men spent all their time doing nothing but loitering in the shops. Some could work the whole day for a pound of meat. They were called the lazy boys and people in the village said that such men would later turn to stealing and crime. This thought always made people shudder because murder in cold-blood was a foul thing. A man who murdered was for ever a curse in heaven and earth. One could recognize such boys because they were to be seen hanging around teashops, meat shops and even in the Indian bazaar, waiting for any errand that might earn them a day's meal. At times they called themselves young Hitlers.

WAGUIH GHALI

EGYPT

Revolutionary Days

From *Beer in the Snooker Club*. The hero of Waguih Ghali's novel is a young Egyptian, Ram, and here he describes his life as a student, involved in a social revolution he only dimly understands. Looking back, he is unable to take himself or the revolution very seriously, and constantly makes fun of both. Yet this is not meant to be merely funny. The author intends us to see something sad as well as amusing about the misdirection of energies, the confusion, the lack of any shape and purpose to Ram's life. It might all be tragic, Ram appears to say, if it weren't so comic: and yet he isn't sure that it *is* comic.

I was just over seventeen when I voted for the first and only time in my life. With my thumb. What I mean is, I pressed my thumb, voluntarily, on an inky pad and then pressed it again, where I was told, on a space next to a name. A boy called Kamal had said: '*Tu veux faire la noce ce soir?*'[1] I had nodded. 'Come over then; best Scotch *et puis on paye en petit poucet*,'[2] I didn't know what '*payer en petit poucet*' meant, but I pretended that I did.

I was at the university then. At last the monotony of school life had ended. The university: strikes, fighting policemen, shouting slogans, stealing sulphur and nitrates from the lab; life at last. And besides, I was in the best of the best—the faculty of medicine. No matter, of course, that my Arabic was deplorable, and that I was, according to a certain Oxford and Cambridge Examination Board, proficient in literature and mathematics but certainly not in biology. No matter that hundreds of much better qualified people queued to be accepted by the faculty. I was one of the privileged; I had strings to pull. Not that I bothered to pull them; my mother, or one of my aunts, must have pulled one from the dangling assortment within her reach. I became: '*Il fait la médecine, ma chère.*'[3]

We killed a certain Zaki Bey. I don't remember who was in power then, I think Nokrashi Pasha, but I know Zaki Bey was head of the police and he came, together with fifty half-starved policemen, to the faculty of medicine. They had a dilapidated tank with them. After a lot of mechanical repairs and consultations, the tank's gun was pointed at us who were on the roof of the faculty's building, and an explosion took place. Some of us extended our hands, trying to catch whatever was emitted from the tank; but it never reached our outstretched hands. It fell, instead, with a thud, on a car belonging to my aunt which I had borrowed that day without permission.

---

[1] 'Do you want to come to a party this evening?'

[2] 'and then we'll pay for it with "Tom Thumb".' The whisky is a bribe and Ram will pay for it with his vote, given by thumbprint.

[3] 'He's studying medicine, my dear.'

This made me very angry indeed. My aunt was bound to know I had taken the car, considering there was now a hole in its roof. I therefore helped catapult a bomb which had just been manufactured on the roof, and Zaki Bey died.

I don't remember which party I voted for, but we were given whisky and salted pea-nuts, after which we were taken in Cadillacs to vote with our thumbs. (Apart from Kamal, none of us was of voting age.)

It was only when I went home that I learnt why Zaki Bey had died. He had ordered the Kasr-el-Nil bridge to be opened while a student demonstration was crossing it, causing death to six. A handsome funeral march, comprising half the police force and thousands of civilians, was organized for him next day. Photographs of the procession were mournfully published in all the evening papers. Among the civilians in the photographs I noticed the presence of a few future brilliant scientists, including Kamal. They were the ones who had manufactured the bomb on the roof of the faculty of medicine the day before.

The usual two-months' closing of the faculty was ordered and most of us went to the beaches of Alexandria.

The university reopened and again I had to choose a political party to belong to. Roughly, there were the following: the Wafd, the Ikhwan (Moslem Brotherhood), the Communists, and the anti-Wafd.

The Wafd paid well provided you were a good orator and organizer of strikes. They gave you a car and, I was told, free drinks at the Arizona or the Auberge—I forget which. The Ikhwan was a fearsome thing to belong to. You could be ordered to shoot anyone at any time in cold blood; they paid you with promises both earthly and otherwise, and you had to be active even when the university was closed (as a Copt, I would not have been able to join that one anyhow). The Communists were the respectable though secretive ones; the hard-working, the intelligent, the quiet. No rewards, only risk of imprisonment and misery to the family. The anti-Wafd was the most popular, and was joined by socialists, anarchists, university-closing fans, semi-idealists, progressives, and most of the middle class.

I didn't join any party, but contented myself with being devoted to 'evacuation' and was always the first home whenever a strike was suggested as a blow to British imperialism.

Kamal came to the lab one afternoon wearing a three-weeks' beard, which meant that he had become a member of the Ikhwan.

'Infidel,' he said, 'can you steal the chemistry storeroom's key today?'

I replied that my examinations were next day and that anyhow I would have nothing to do with the Ikhwan. He said that although he had recently joined the Ikhwan, this was a job for the last party to which he had belonged. He then wrote down seven examination questions, telling me to expect them in next day's paper. I started to tell him that I didn't need the questions, thank you very much, then I gave a bit of a start; the questions he gave me were all very different from those I had bought for twenty-five pounds the day before. Furthermore, it would have taken me at least three days to prepare the answers to the questions he had just given me. A mistake, it seemed, had been made. Rewards had been given to the wrong students.

Next morning I walked rather dejectedly to the examination hall; I would barely be able to answer three out of the seven questions. I was greeted with the news that the examination hall had been burnt down and that examinations would be postponed for ten days at least.

Kamal's picture next appeared in the procession consequent to the killing of Nokrashi Pasha, and also in that following the killing of Sheikh-el-Banna, head of the Ikhwan. Just before the revolution Kamal owned two cars, a villa on the Pyramid Road, and a flat in town. I met him once after the revolution.

He was riding a number six tram to Shubra, a handkerchief round his neck to protect his collar, wearing an old brown suit and brown plimsolls.

'My market has been closed,' he said sadly after a flowery greeting. 'You infidel,' he added with a smile.

DRISS BEN HAMED CHARHADI
MOROCCO

Prison Break

From *A Life Full of Holes*, an unusual book, since its author cannot read or write. When the novelist, Paul Bowles, was on holiday in Morocco he became friendly with an illiterate working man, who was at first puzzled and then fascinated by the idea of 'making a book'. After a while, the man, Driss ben Hamed Charhadi, asked whether he could make a book of his own by telling it into a tape recorder, and this is how *A Life Full of Holes* came to be written. Paul Bowles translated it from the Moghrebi Arabic in which it was first composed.

When this episode opens, Charhadi is in jail for selling drugs, and the prisoners are planning to escape.

One day I heard a man named Chaib talking to another in the courtyard. He was saying: Now, you've got two years and that one there has three. Each one of us has a lot of time to stay in jail. And now Ramadan's here and we're going to spend the festival in jail. And the Sultan is coming to town for the feast, and we won't see him or anything.

The other one said: And what are we going to do about it, here in prison?

We can do one thing, said Chaib.

What's that?

Escape.

Escape? How are we going to do that?

We can grab the guards and tie them up. There aren't many guards here. Only five. That's nothing. Look how many of us there are. If everybody agrees on it, we can all escape.

The other one said: Yes. But we'd have to ask everybody here about it.

And they began to talk about it. Every time we walked in the courtyard those two men would talk to the prisoners who had long sentences to serve. Chaib would say to them: Do you want to get out? And they would say: Yes, if I find somebody to help me. And Chaib would tell them: You've got this one and that one and the others. He would give them the names of all the men he had already talked to and who had agreed on it.

This is what we're going to do and this is how we're going to do it, he would tell them. Ouakha, they would say. And Chaib went on talking to the prisoners and they all said: Yes, yes. Then he told them: There are two Nazarenes here who have a long time to stay in prison. I'm going to ask them, too. If they want to get out with us, good.

Chaib could get into the courtyard where the Nazarene prisoners were, because the chief trusted him and let him go everywhere inside the jail. The rest of us saw the Nazarenes only when they came to take a bath.

The others said that was good, if the two Nazarenes wanted to go with them. Chaib went to the courtyard where they were, and he talked to the two men. One was a Galician who had eight years, and one was a German who had twenty.

One night we were all talking together in the cell. Chaib, I said, that tall Nazarene, who is he?

That's the German. He's the one who killed his woman at El Aaqaba el Hamra.

Yes, I said. And who was the woman?

She came with him from Germany to work with him here in politics.

And why did he kill her?

Because she fell in love with somebody else. She wouldn't go with him any more. She didn't even like to talk with him.

How could anybody kill a woman for nothing? I said. That's nothing, what she did.

That's the way Nazarenes are, he said. If a woman doesn't like a man or something, he can kill her just for that.

How did he kill her? I asked him.

Just with rocks. He took her in his car out there to the mountains. They got out and were talking. He picked up a rock and said to her: Do you know how much this stone weighs? She said: How much? Six or seven kilos, he told her. Take it in your hand and see. She took the rock in her hand. It's heavy, she told him. Then she handed it back to him. He took it and banged it against her head. She fell down. Then he took other rocks and threw them at her. He kept throwing them until she was all covered up. When none of her showed under the pile of rocks, he got into the car and drove back to the Hotel Rif. And they caught him, and brought him here. And he's got twenty years.

He deserves them, I said. Because that woman did nothing bad to him. He had no right to kill her like that.

And so Chaib went to the courtyard of the Nazarenes and talked to the German. We're going to escape, he told him, and if you want to go with us, good. We're going to get everything ready first and all leave together. Do you want to come?

Yes, said the German. I'll go with you, beat anybody you say, do anything you want.

Good, said Chaib. But we've got to tell Miguel the Gallego.

It's better not to say anything to that one, the German told him. He's not going to be able to escape anyway.

Ouakha, said Chaib.

When are you going to do all this? asked the German.

Wait. In another two days or so I'll tell you.

That day went by. The next day Chaib was talking to every-body. You know, he said, tomorrow's Thursday, visitors' day. Each of you who has visitors tomorrow must ask them to bring some clothes on Saturday.

And so each one of us asked his friends and family to bring him street clothes so that no one would be wearing jail clothes after we escaped. Aicha came with her daughter, and I asked her to bring me some sandals and a pair of trousers. She said she would. But you must bring them Saturday, I told her.

Why do you want them Saturday? You've got sandals on.

Yes, but they're broken. Anyway, please bring them Saturday.

And she brought everything and gave it to the guard. He called me. Hamed! Here. Take this package. It's for you.

That night when we were all in our cell we were talking together about the hour we were going to escape the next day. We had to be sure that every prisoner understood the exact time when it was going to happen. Tomorrow is Sunday, they are saying, and the guards on duty will be Cherif el Abbar, he's an old man, and Bba Miloud the Algerian, and two Nazarenes. And one more outside makes five. They're all old and married, with families, so they'll be afraid when we grab them.

But how are we going to do it? they were asking.

Hapot and Amar Riffi will begin to fight in the courtyard, the guard there will yell at them and try to separate them, and we'll grab him then.

Ouakha, ouakha, they said.

Now we won't save any more food, said Chaib. We'll eat everything tonight. Everyone brought out the butter and the oil he had been saving, and we rolled pieces of rags and dipped them in the oil and butter. Then we set the rags on fire and cooked our food over them. Whoever had tea or sugar or milk brought it out. And if a man had nothing, the others gave what they had to him. We did not want to leave anything there. All night we cooked and ate and smoked kif in the dark, until the cannon went off an hour before dawn. Then we all went to bed before it got light. A little later the guards came and knocked on the door. Get up! Get up!

And we got up. Each man put his street clothes on under his overalls. At nine o' clock we went out into the courtyard and began to walk around, the same as every day. In a little while Hapot and Amar Riffi started to fight with each other. The old guard Cherif el Abbar went to stop them, but when he got near them all the prisoners grabbed him. One of them hit him on the head with a rock. If he had hit him a little harder he would have killed him. They dragged him into a cell and threw him on the floor and shut the door. Then they ran to the office and saw Bba Miloud there. Some of the men got frightened then and began to run back, but the others cried: Go on! Go on, you Jews! Are you afraid? Then everybody went ahead.

Bba Miloud ran out to the other courtyard. One of the Spanish guards was standing there. When the Spaniard saw him with all the prisoners running behind him, he went into the nearest cell and locked the door. I was in the office and I saw the German come running and take the telephone in his hands. He pulled the wire out of the wall and threw the telephone on the floor. Another prisoner broke off the head of a bottle and ran to cut Bba Miloud with it. I grabbed his arm and stopped him. No! No! he's the best guard in the jail, I told him. Be careful. If you kill him it'll be bad for you. Leave him and let's go. Then Bba Miloud took a big bunch of keys out of his pocket and threw them over the wall into the garden outside.

The German found a ladder and climbed to the top of the wall and jumped over. Then a lot of men took a plank and began to ram it against the door. The third time they hit it, it broke open. Half the prisoners ran out. The others were still in the office looking for money and other things to steal.

Between the men's and the women's courtyards there was

a wall with a grill in it. One of the women guards began to shout: Don't break things! Don't break anything! Just go out! Just run! Run!

And they were breaking all the windows and tables, and throwing bottles of medicine and books and typewriters on the floor. And they tore up all the papers and threw them up into the air. Everything. It looked like the war.

There was a guard outside by the electric generator. When he saw what was happening he tried to take his pistol out of his pocket, but before he could get it out the prisoners threw rocks at him and he fell down. Everybody threw more rocks on top of him, and then they smashed the generator. Chaib was shouting: Come on! The door's open! Go on out! He went to El Mernissi's window and said: Wait. I'll get the key and let you out. But El Mernissi told him: No! No! I don't want to go out. You just go.

The woman was still yelling: No! Don't hit anybody! Run! Run! Then the prisoners broke the other door, the one that is on the highway, and they began to run out that way.

The guard who was outside was holding his head where they had hit him, and he was crying: Ay, yimma el habiba! Everybody was running, and I ran out the door with the others. It was raining hard then, and the mud was deep everywhere. I decided to go on the highway. I forgot to take off my overalls, and I began to run with them on. A little later I saw the truck coming from the city to bring water to the jail. Allah! I thought. Now they're going to catch us all! The truck's going to get to the jail and they're going to see what's happened and go back to tell the police. I'm going to take the river and cut through to Tanja el Balia. That will bring me out into Beni Makada. That was where Aicha and her daughter lived.

I was going along the edge of the river. I turned around and saw the German running behind me. I made signs with my hand: Come on! He had one bad foot. He would run a little, and then he would stop and wait. He was carrying a leather case in his hand. I waited for him. Here, he said. Take this bag, please, and carry it for me.

Ouakha, I said. Give it to me. I began to run again. My feet were going deep into the mud and water, and I was getting tired. I left the river and ran across the fields, and he was following me. Then I came to another stream, and I thought it was shallow so I could get across it, but there was a deep part there, and I went down into it. The water was up to my neck.

Ya latif! I thought. This is trouble! If I'd known it was going to be like this, I'd have stayed in jail. The German gave me his hand and pulled me out of the water, and we began to run again. Then I shouted to him: I'm sick of this. Here's your bag! Take care of it yourself.

I threw the bag into a pile of brambles and ran ahead by myself. I kept running, running, until I came out onto the road. There I saw another prisoner named Hamouda who had escaped too. He was yelling: Run! Run! The soldiers are coming!

I was very tired from running. We got to the ruins of the Portuguese Fort by the road that goes to Tanja el Balia. We hid inside the ruins while the soldiers went by. It was raining hard, but from where we were we could see the road all the way back to the jail. There are no trees or houses out there. The trucks stopped in front of the jail and the soldiers began to go in all directions through the fields and over the hills behind, looking for the prisoners. And they found a lot of them and were taking them back into the jail.

We went into the village of Tanja el Balia and came out behind the power plant. Then we cut across to the abattoir, climbed around the side of the hill, and came out by the bull-ring. It was not raining any more. From there Hamouda and I went to Beni Makada, to the house where Aicha lived.

PETRO KILEKWA

ZAMBIA

The Slave-Dhow

From *Slave Boy to Priest*. Petro Kilekwa was born in N. Rhodesia, now Zambia, about eighty years ago, but carried off by Arab slave traders while he was still only a boy. Fortunately, the ship transporting him into slavery was captured by a British naval vessel, and he was released. This incident is described in the following episode from his autobiography, translated from the Nyanja by K. H. Nixon Smith.

On the third evening we saw a big dhow and that same night we all went on board and all the slaves were placed on the lower deck. We travelled all night and in the morning we found that we were in the midst of the sea and out of sight of land. We went on thus for many days over the sea. At first we had food twice a day, in the morning and in the evening. The men had two platefuls and the women two and for our relish we often had fish, for our masters the Arabs caught a large number of fish with hooks and line. But because the journey was so long the food began to run short and so we were hungry, and also water was short and they began to mix it with sea water.

After a long time at sea we drew near to land and we went on shore to try to get food and water. We stayed on shore one day and we got a little food and some water. The next day we pushed off. On the third say we heard our masters the Arabs exclaiming: 'Land, land! Muscat.' But we passed on without landing because the wind was high and our vessel was driven into a harbour in the Persian Gulf.

In the morning about nine o'clock the Arabs began to order us to go down to the lower deck, and those who were un-willing to leave the upper deck were shut in the centre of the lower deck and we were told, 'Europeans are coming! They have sighted us. Their boat is a long way off. They do not want us Arabs, certainly not, but they are after you slaves and they will eat you and they will grind your bones and make sweetmeats of them. Europeans are much whiter than we Arabs are—hide yourselves.'

All the time the vessel kept moving. We did not stop for an instant, till we heard, 'Lower the sail,' and they began to lower it. At that time some of the Arabs grasped their swords and one man had a gun. The European boat overtook us quickly and drew up close to our dhow. And one Arab began to dance about with his sword in hand but the other Arabs stopped him. The Europeans demanded, 'Have you any slaves on board?' and the Arabs answered 'No, we have not any.' However, a European and some black men came on board and searched for us, and officers and sailors were ready in their boat with guns and cutlasses so that if any of the Arabs made trouble they could fight with them. A European and a black man peered down into the lower deck and saw us slaves, ever so many of us, and when we saw the face of the European we were terrified. We were quite certain that Europeans eat people but the European said to the black man: 'Tell them not to be afraid but let them rejoice', and the European began to smile and to laugh. And the sailor and the black man told the other Europeans who were on the boat, 'There are slaves here, ever so many of them.'

At once the officers and sailors began to climb into our dhow with cutlasses in their hands. And the officers said to the Arabs: 'Lay down your swords and your guns, if you offer any resistance you will all be killed.' Thereupon they laid down their swords and they were at once put on board the European boat, and other European sailors brought us up to the top deck. Then they got ropes and fastened our dhow to their boat and they rowed gently along with us in our dhow till we came to a small island at evening time and they landed us there.

There was a camp on the island and some tins there, but not very many. Our masters opened them and began to give us biscuits. When we tried to eat them, we found that they were very dry, but while we were eating them our masters brought us fresh water to drink. Our dhow they tied up on shore with ropes. We were about two days on the island and on the third day we saw something dazzling and white out at sea with three masts and some cross beams, and smoke was coming out of it. We got into a panic instantly and thought our death was near and that our bones would be made into sweetmeats, but the sailors we were with on the island were delighted and told us not to be afraid and they said: 'Look, that's our flag and our home on the water; it travels up and down.' The vessel came slowly along to the island and we saw that it was very large. That vessel was Her Majesty's Ship *Osprey*.

We were ordered at once to line up in the harbour and boats came alongside to take us on board. The women were taken first to the ship and then we men and boys were put on deck. After that the Arabs who had been our masters were brought on board the ship, but they were kept by themselves because they were prisoners. When we had all got on board, we looked towards the island and we saw that our dhow was on fire, for the captain had ordered the sailors to set it on fire. Before the ship put off the sailors came with buckets of water for us to wash in but the water was salt. They tried washing us with soap and rubbing us down but the soap would hardly lather. When we had washed we saw dishes of rice and brown sugar. Some of us thought that the Europeans were tricking us and that they meant to fatten us, so that they might eat us and make our bones into sweetmeats. And we thought that the brown sugar which they gave us was made out of the bones of our fellows who had been captured before us.

That same day in the evening, or perhaps it was in the night time, after we were all on board the man-of-war,

H.M.S. *Osprey* sailed all night, coming from the Persian coast and making for Muscat in Arabia, and we arrived there in the early morning. The British consul was at Muscat and he came on board the man-of-war to look at us, and he arranged with the captain to land us on the mainland. We got into boats to go there. They led us to a big enclosure with a high wall round it behind the house of the British consul. We never heard what had become of the Arabs who had been our masters.

Muscat was at that time a large town belonging to the Arabs, and the Sultan lived there, and we saw a number of Africans at work in the town and in the harbour. The British consul was in charge of the English quarter. I think his duty was to receive and care for rescued slaves who had been freed. We liked living in the enclosure very much indeed; we had clothes given us made of cotton and everyone's cloth was the right size for him and the food was good; we had dates or onions in the morning and in the daytime we had rice and in the evening rice again, with a relish of fish or meat. And we all danced in the evenings the dances which we used to dance in our village. We forgot all our fears when we were slaves and expecting to be killed and eaten and to have our bones made into sugar by the Europeans, but we felt sad about being far from our relations and our homes and we wondered what our end would be.

CYPRIAN EKWENSI

NIGERIA

Jagua's Love-Letter

From *Jagua Nana*. This extract raises a question which you have been asked to think about elsewhere in the anthology—must all good literature be written in good English? And in order to answer this, you'll have to think about what you mean by good English, since the best authors sometimes use forms of English which are ungrammatical or 'incorrect' in some way. For example, if a character in a play or novel is supposed to be an uneducated man, the author can hardly let him use educated English. If he did, you'd probably criticize the book on the grounds that this character was not portrayed convincingly. So when we speak of 'good' English in literature, we don't necessarily mean 'correct' English according to the grammar book, but the English which best creates the effect aimed at by the author. Everyone uses a language in many different ways according to the circumstances in which he is using it—making a speech in a political debate, addressing a jury in court, applying for a job, writing a letter to a girl-friend, drinking with friends in a bar. A good writer must be very conscious of these different styles, or registers of the language, using them correctly or else deliberately misusing them to amuse or shock the reader.

Here, then, we have Jagua Nana, an illiterate woman in love, and we have the Letter-Writer, whose English is far from perfect. Between them they are composing a letter to Jagua's boy-friend in England, Freddie, and the author reveals them to us through the kind of language which they would use if they were people in real life. The letter uses the worn phrases of love—'a land of dream', 'my heart and soul were aflame', 'your heavenly eyes' and so on—but its clumsiness is dramatic, the character's clumsiness not the author's. In this way, the letter is able to convey the strong feelings which lie beneath its inadequate language, and the reader can be moved by Jagua's efforts to express what she cannot find words for. We recognize that there is irony when the author tells us that 'the beautiful words, she felt, fully conveyed her feelings', but this also makes us aware of her seriousness and her humanity.

In her elegant *Accra*-style blouse and *lappa*, Jagua sat on a packing case, crossed her dainty shoes and held a sparkling yellow-green sun umbrella above her head. She had been speaking to the rusty-haired old man for a while when he looked up and beamed through his glasses. He handled her words like a priest at the confessional, each one with a sense of the power to save or perish the soul, to shower with happiness of flood with sorrow. The Letter-Writer had developed the benign air of forgiveness for youthful intrepidity—a quality which attracted Jagua and made her confide intimate stories to him. At the end of the session, Jagua realized that she had told him nearly everything there was to know about Freddie. At the same time, a sharper definition of her relationship with Freddie emerged.

'Gently, gently, I soon write dat one down.' The old Letter-Writer dipped his pen in the ink-bottle, waved it about in the air, in diminishing circles till the point of the nib made contact with the paper. 'Eheh?...Eheh?...And den...Go on!'

Jagua was short of ideas. 'Read what you got down.'

She could not fully understand the whole of what he read, but she knew when a letter sounded right, and this one did. The beautiful words, she felt, fully conveyed her feelings and she loved the Letter-Writer for his cleverness. Before he read it out to her, he took off his glasses, polished them, and replaced them. He put the sheet of paper a good distance away and read:

My Darling Freddie,

I remembered the very day you left me for England, I was charmed by your beautiful face which took me to a land of dream at the very night; you know where hearts agree there joy will be, your love attracted me; my heart and soul were aflame, the love in you cannot be abolished by any human creature except God the Almighty. I last night dreamt of your beautiful and your smiling face which seems to me like vision.

Look, dear one, I am specially moved by feelings from heart to heart to love you always dearly and I hope you will have some love for me through your long stay in that cold firmament the United Kingdom.

I will be always loving you and adoring you with all my heart till you return. There's nothing lives longer than love, which sends perfect happiness to the soul, therefore will you summon your beautiful strength and body to me as I am dreaming on my side. God's ways are mysterious, nobody knows Him or His contemplation on the end. Therefore let us live lonely and happily as you know, you are a nobleman and charming among your fellows, don't you see God creates you a part of them? And I am proud of you in all respect, for God knows the way we must treat, and could not hope for a finer example.

With all my heart-soul love and hoping to hear from you again as early as possible.

With true love and affection wishing you happiness till once more I look into your heavenly eyes and hearing your sonorous voice...

Hand on chin, Jagua listened, sighing, nodding.

'Das all I got down.' The old Letter-Writer looked up.

'I got nothing more to say, sah. Tell him Cheerio. May God Bless am wherever he may go. Den I kin sign.'

EDWARD ATIYAH

LEBANON/SUDAN

One Hump or Two

From *Black Vanguard*. A Sudanese sheikh and his Oxford-educated son have just returned from London to the Sudan, and a gathering is being held in their honour. The author, Edward Atiyah, is an Arab from the Lebanon, but he lived in the Sudan for twenty-five years, first of all as a lecturer in History, and then as Government Public Relations Officer. This extract from the novel needs no comment, except perhaps to explain the surprise of the guests at the story of the camel with two humps. The African camel or dromedary, the kind they know, has only one hump, and the kind in London Zoo which had two was an Asian Camel.

The news spread quickly that Sheikh Ahmed and his son had returned. A kind of verbal rediffusion system operated in the town whereby the news of arrivals, deaths and other sudden social phenomena reached almost everybody by the evening of the day of their occurrence. Many friends had met them at the station, but that did not render a congratulatory visit to the house unnecessary, and there were hundreds of acquaintances who must also come as soon as they heard. In the town there was no social hierarchy, no rigid boundaries between different income or culture levels. Everybody who was not 'rabble' knew everybody else, and important private events were often like a public function in which everybody parti-

cipated. If in a house of mourning the people of the deceased
were of modest means, friends and neighbours sent contribu-
tions of coffee and sugar to help cope with the hundreds who
came to condole and to whom coffee must be served. Often,
chairs and carpets had to be borrowed. Even in Sheikh Ahmed's
house it was deemed necessary to import a few extra settees
for the occasion, and these with the entire seating equipment
of the house were arranged in a large square round the garden
and along the verandahs and terraces. All the carpets, too,
were brought out at sunset and spread on the terraces, for
many of the visitors would prefer to sit on the ground, taking
off their red slippers and depositing them with their canes in
a heap near the steps as they came in.

Soon after dark they began to arrive, and rapidly the garden
filled up. Everybody came. The big merchants and small shop-
keepers of the market-place, senior and junior Government
officials, the men of religion, the teachers of all the schools,
college students who had been at school with Mahmoud, the
editors of the five papers, Sheikh Ayyoub and his son, the
judge, Mustapha Effendi and Osman and the doctor. About
half of them were in European clothes. A few wore beautiful
robes and belts like Sheikh Ahmed's. But the rest came in their
long white shirts and turbans, with a black cloak carried care-
lessly across their shoulders. They carried rustic sticks, and
on their bare feet wore the traditional red slippers with the
figure-three toe-cap. Even the district judge, who usually wore
a suit, came this evening in this native costume, billowing in
it freely, saying he had found it too hot to wear anything
else.

They sat round the square, in chairs close to one another,
and on the verandahs, but even before the chairs filled up some
started sitting cross-legged on the carpets, and the heap of
slippers near the edge of the terrace began to grow. Sheikh
Ahmed and Mahmoud had to rise constantly to welcome the

new arrivals, who might be a solitary walker, or somebody who had just tethered a donkey outside, or a bunch coming out of a car. Some came in quietly, uttering a taciturn perfunctory greeting; others, like the district judge, blew in on a tide of laughter, prepared to wrench your arm out of its socket with the reiterated warmth of their greeting. Trays of lemonade went round, then trays of coffee. The judge was very thirsty, asked for a second bucket-tumbler of lemonade, and under moderate pressure from Sheikh Ahmed, took a third, saying by way of apology, 'A curse upon onions and garlic... God forgive you, Osman, for that lunch you gave us!' The spectators watched the three glassfuls vanish in the immense interior, poured in rather than gulped.

Not many people from the country had visited England. One or two deputations had gone there on political missions, but Sheikh Ahmed and his son were the first to have had the experience as private individuals. Everybody wanted to hear from them something about it. Nor was Sheikh Ahmed's anxiety to impart less than theirs to receive. He imparted lavishly; and from time to time, summing up each item, he said:

'Beyond doubt, a great country and a great people.'

'Don't they despise a black skin?' asked Mustapha Effendi.

'By God, I came across nothing but courtesy wherever I went. They're very decent to foreigners. We stayed at the Savoy Hotel, the greatest in London, and had the best treatment you could imagine. Also in the shops, at railway stations, everywhere...No, no. They are a very polite people in their country.'

'In their country,' said a young nationalist, with significant emphasis.

'But one hears of incidents,' said Osman, '...black men being refused admission to hotels or restaurants. It happens quite often.'

'You are thinking of America,' said the doctor, 'and of South Africa. I don't think England is like that.'

'It happens sometimes in England,' said Mahmoud. 'It never happened to me, but I heard of cases. It is rare though, and funnily enough it never happens to anybody in native costume, because they think he is a prince or something. It is only black men in European clothes who come across it.' There was a general laugh, and one of the contingent in traditional robes said:

'How splendid! Then we should all be princes there!'

'Perhaps,' said the doctor, 'they mistake black men in European clothes for American negroes.'

'And why should they be prejudiced against American negroes in England?' asked Osman.

'They've caught the infection from their American cousins,' said the judge. 'They think because they are despised in America, they must be inferior.'

Sheikh Ayyoub cleared his throat and, turning in his chair, expectorated a bullet into the saucer bed of a lontana shrub a few paces away. Then he said, addressing Mahmoud, 'But you and Amin at Oxford, you were treated exactly like the sons of the English, isn't that so?'

'Of course,' said Mahmoud. 'At the college, in the university, there was no difference at all, and we had many good friends, though some of the students were not too keen to mix with us, and in the town one met sometimes people that were not very agreeable, but it did not worry us. Mr Barry, the headmaster of the English school, had warned us about it in a nice way before we went there. He told us, "You must know that there are stupid people in England as everywhere else, and that one form of their narrow-mindedness is a dislike of foreigners, particularly if their colour is different from their own. You must not mind it. These people are not worth bothering about."'

'Admirable and beautiful words,' said Mustapha Effendi.

'No doubt about it; a great people in their country,' said Sheikh Ahmed.

'Why don't they stay in their country, then, and leave other people alone?' said Osman, *sotto voce*, but Sheikh Ahmed heard him. He said, 'By God, Osman, if you want the truth and not its cousin, they are a great people even here. Leave nonsense and newspaper talk aside; this is the truth, and we still need them.'

'True, true,' said a number of voices from nodding heads.

'But will they know when we have ceased to need them, brothers? That's the crux and that's the trouble. They won't. Have you heard of their ever doing it anywhere?'

'Let us wait till then,' said Sheikh Ahmed. 'If they don't, and you come out with your gun, I will come out with mine, and for every Englishman you kill, I will kill five.'

'But in the meantime,' said Osman, 'you are standing for the Assembly?'

'Maybe.'

The judge, who knew both Sheikh Ahmed and Osman well, sensed the rumblings of a storm, and thought it best to divert the conversation from this political channel. He said, 'What were the things in England that struck you most, the things that one going from here would find least familiar?'

Sheikh Ahmed told them about social discipline and honesty, about queues and punctuality, and how the newspaperman trusted you to buy your paper in his absence and drop your coin in an open box in the street, which nobody thought of rifling. And he told them about the London police and the traffic and the Underground, and the uncanny precision of a balance in the Bank of England which could register the weight of the ink used in writing a single word on a sheet of paper. Then he laughed and said, 'But this is all nothing. Do you want to know what was really the most amazing thing I saw in England?...It was a camel with two humps!'

An uproar of excited exclamations, questions and adjurations by Allah greeted this astounding statement. All the rest they had accepted without question, in silent marvelling, because it was not of their world—but the camel! Why, they knew everything there was to be known about camels, yet they had never seen one with two humps. The thing could not exist; and in spite of Sheikh Ahmed's solemn assurances and repeated descriptions of the dromedary he had seen at the London Zoo, some of the older visitors left without entirely surrendering their scepticism.

THOMAS MOFOLO

BASUTOLAND

The Death of Noliwe

From *Chaka: An Historical Romance*. At this point in the epic of Chaka's career, he is close to achieving supreme power amongst the Zulu people by skill in war and diplomacy. But in Mofolo's account, Chaka is corrupted by this power and grows more and more unscrupulous and tyrannical. His witch-doctor, Isanusi, has told him that if he marries the girl Noliwe, he cannot rise any higher in authority; but if he wishes for the greatest honours, he must be prepared to sacrifice Noliwe—sacrifice her literally by killing her. Chaka gives his decision to Isanusi in these words: 'Truth to tell, there is nothing on earth except only the chieftainship, war, and my regiments. And therefore I will give thee Noliwe, that all hindrances may be removed from my path to the chieftainship. I have deliberated and made an end; the medicines shall be compounded of the blood of Noliwe.' But Chaka is a Macbeth-like figure, torn between ambition and conscience, and the killing of Noliwe is not as easy a matter as his decision makes it sound.

The months for reflection appointed by Isanusi came to an end, and Chaka's decision was not altered; he stood where he did before. As we have said already, there was one great obstacle to Chaka's marriage, namely, to whom should he give the cattle?[1] For it was obvious that he could not take Noliwe in marriage for nothing, as if she were a wastrel. All the same, Chaka continued to visit Noliwe and she became pregnant. And now she longed for Chaka's love, and always wept if she could not see him.

And Chaka loved Noliwe in return; she was the one person we could imagine Chaka as loving, if he loved any woman with sincerity. All that is good, all that is beautiful, all that any true wife can give her husband, Chaka would have got from Noliwe if from anyone. And although he was bartering her away in this fashion and was planning to kill her, yet his conscience troubled him, and gave him no rest, telling him always that he had descended from the level of a man. But because of the chieftainship he smothered his conscience and pressed on, bearing death on his shoulders.

It was beginning to be clear that the methods used by Ndlebe and Malunga were without any doubt leading him to the chieftainship that he desired, and so he swallowed his fears and hardened his heart.

Malunga told him that the period promised had already passed, and that doubtless Isanusi had allowed it to pass on purpose so that Chaka might be fixed in his resolve. Then Chaka said: 'But the delay of Isanusi will embarrass me, for I am eager now to go to war. We have been here doing naught for a long time, and the rust will eat into our spears.'

Malungi said: 'Yea, but according to the way I have been working thou canst not go to war without shedding the blood of the one that thou dost love, and *that* is Isanusi's part not mine. If after deliberation thou sparest Noliwe, *I* can do

---

[1] Noliwe was the sister of Dingiswayo, who had died and been succeeded by Chaka. Thus Chaka was both her guardian, the one to receive the cattle, and her lover, the one who should give the cattle.

naught. It is Isanusi alone that can undo what I have done. He only it is who can both go forward and go back, who can do and undo.' Chaka heard and he understood that it was still possible to have mercy on Noliwe and spare her, and his thoughts were troubled.

The evening of that day Isanusi arrived and went to them in the hut, and Chaka and he were alone, and broached the question: 'How is it with thee Chaka? Hast thou decided to live with Noliwe as thy wife as was determined by Dingiswayo and his tribe and also by thee, or hast thou determined to win the chieftainship?'

'I, Chaka, know not how to make my tongue say two different things. What I have said I have said, Isanusi.' Isanusi remained silent for a long while and gazed on the ground. At last he raised his head and said, 'Greeting, my kinsmen. Malunga, how is it with thee? Hast thou done thy work?'

'I have done it and I have finished, Isanusi. We are waiting but for thee, whose part it is to complete and to finish.'

Isanusi said: 'The medicine has been given to the warriors and they have not known of it?' 'It has been given, Isanusi.' 'The spears have been newly forged and prepared in the proper manner, as are the spears of the warriors of our country?' 'They have been forged, and they have been prepared, Isanusi.' 'The medicines have been correctly mixed?' 'They have been correctly mixed, Isanusi. All that thou didst command have I done in the way that thou commandest it and have finished.' Isanusi turned to Ndlebe and said, 'Ndlebe, what hast thou done since I departed?'

'I have prepared with drugs the hearts of the people, of the men and of the women, so that whatever Chaka may do they will perceive is right, because it is done by Chaka—Chaka who was sent by the Gods unto men. Further, I have given them of Forgetfulness to eat so that where there was doubt they may forget it and be without understanding, so that they may see naught, but look only to Chaka and regard him as they regard Nkulunkulu.' Isanusi smiled and said, 'Thou hast worked well in a weighty matter.' Then Isanusi again asked Chaka the question that he had just asked him, and Chaka gave the same answer as before. Again Isanusi was silent for a long time and was perplexed like a judge unwilling to condemn one whom he loved, yet bound by circumstances to condemn him and to pass a hard sentence—against his will.

And then Isanusi said: 'Think well, Chaka. What has been done by my servants can be undone, but that which I will do through the blood of Noliwe, thy wife, even I cannot undo. What will be done will be done for ever. Therefore a man must understand what he doth while there is yet time, lest afterwards he repent and it is of no avail. When I departed from thee I told thee that to-day we would teach thee the innermost secrets of witchcraft, and so it is; for we are witch-doctors mightier than all others. If thou dost determine to win the chieftainship, thou wilt become a different man and be like unto the chiefs of our country. But I will ask thee yet again and do thou answer speaking the truth that is in thy heart and fear nothing, fear not even that I shall weary thee again to no purpose. Which dost thou choose—Noliwe, or the chieftainship?'

And Chaka answered, 'The chieftainship.'

In the twinkling of an eye Isanusi's brow cleared and lit up and the gloom that had enveloped him fled and gave place to joy, and he said: 'Thou hast answered like a man after my own heart. I have no patience with one whose thoughts waver. With these questions I tested thee to know the depth of thy under-standing and I see that thou art a man: when thou hast spoken, thou hast spoken. Thou art a chief and thy answer is the answer of a chief. To-day I know what thou art, and I will work with a joyful heart even more than before, since I know thy nature. Through the death of Noliwe thou wilt learn of many things, and though thou wilt not discover them at once thou wilt discover them later. Thou shalt learn, too, that there is no death, there is no destruction. When it is said that a man has died he has not died but has been changed; the breath of his life has left this dry skin that is his body, and has gone to another land that is more glorious than the sun, and he goeth to live there retaining his true nature, even as thou hast heard the voice of thy father speaking with thee—and it was he himself that spoke. He that hath worked well on earth will reap a rich harvest there; he that hath done naught here reapeth naught there, for all that a man doth here the sun when it sets takes with it to that great city of the living, the city of those who, *ye* say, have died and are dead. And his acts await him there, ever growing, ever increasing, like the cattle that bring forth calves each year. But if a man has done little, his acts instead of increasing decrease and diminish. It is with him as with a man that hath ploughed little, and when he saith he will thresh his few ears of corn that are but a handful, instead of an abundance they fill but one small leathern bag or are lost amid the dust of the threshing floor, and he is left destitute and empty-handed.

'Even now thou art about to enter in to the number of the mighty, yea, even the mighty that I see even now where they dwell, surrounded by the glory of their works, they who were men, who strove and laboured in their day, and wrought manfully. Even now thou art about to enter into the number of the chiefs who are like unto the chiefs of our land.' Then Isanusi began to be sad and was silent as if he were on the point of revealing to Chaka the secrets of the land beyond the grave. Chaka listened to all this with eagerness and excitement and with an urgent longing to reach soon a chieftainship of such a kind.

Then Isanusi continued and said: 'Thou art a man of understanding, Chaka; truly there are not many like unto thee for knowing the times. For there is a time in the life of man which, if it pass him and leave him, then fortune has passed him by, such fortune as he will never see again until he comes to lie in the cold earth. But if he give heed to the time and perceive it, he can win a happiness that will never again elude him. One such time was when I found thee asleep under the bush: if thou hadst not chosen manhood then, where wouldst thou have been?' (And Chaka said to himself, 'Indeed where should I have been?')

'To-day is another such time. Thou hast known how to choose the path along which thou wilt walk and the way in which thou wilt live on earth, and when thou diest thy king- dom will be without limits. And greatest of all, thy fame and the glory of thy reign—thou wilt find it all there increased tenfold among thy fathers when thou comest to them, and it will be for ever and ever; for there is no death: there men live for ever according as they have lived here on earth.' Isanusi was again silent for a long while and then he drew Chaka to him and they went outside where he looked up at the sky and pointed to the stars: 'The number of thy warriors will soon be greater than the multitudinous stars thou seest in the heavens. Among the tribes thou wilt shine as doth the sun when no clouds cover it, before which when it riseth the stars disappear. And before thee, too, the tribes will indeed disappear when thou appearest, for the blood of Noliwe will bring to thee untold riches.'

The reader can imagine what were the thoughts of Chaka when he was promised such fame and such glory, and was promised them by the one whom he knew to speak the truth in all things. Nevertheless, things remained as they were for a few days and nothing was done; they were waiting till near the time when Chaka should go down in the morning to the river, so that the deed might be done then.

The next day Chaka, after he returned from watching his

regiments drill, found that Isanusi and his attendants were no longer there but had gone to procure medicines from the veld and the bush. He entered Noliwe's hut and found her alone with her servant girl, and at once when he saw her he discovered that she had a beautiful brown colour, her skin was smooth and shining, and her beauty was overpowering. There was a look of tenderness in her sparkling eyes. Her voice, when she spoke to Chaka her beloved, far suppressed in his ears the war songs and praises which he had persuaded himself were so beautiful. The tone of her voice was beautifully pitched, clear yet soft, and full of sincerity without guile or deceit. But above all, her eyes, which so clearly said, 'I am thine, Chaka, my whole self is thine, in life and in death.' At that moment her beauty made him dumb, so that he could not speak, but stood there powerless. He rubbed his eyes and looked away, and when he looked at Noliwe again he found that her beauty was greater than ever; it was a beauty befitting the woman so dearly loved by Nkulunkulu who had been chosen out by him to show to men the perfection of womanhood. In Chaka's mind a whirlwind seemed to spring up, a mighty tempest shook him and the dust flew: then he went. When Isanusi returned he said to him, even before Chaka spoke:'Thou art a man indeed, Chaka. I saw the confusion of thy thoughts when thou didst look upon Noliwe, but thou holdest to thy manhood like a chief, for a chief should not vary his purposes from day to day.'

As Chaka's day approached Noliwe sickened, for she was pregnant, and she was suffering from her burden, although her pregnancy was not yet so advanced that people would take notice. On the evening before Chaka was to go down to the pool Chaka went to her, taking with him a long needle of the kind used for sewing grain baskets. He found her sitting alone with only her handmaiden, in order to be quiet, and as he entered the handmaiden went out. There was a fire of wood burning and its flames provided a bright light which lit up the hut.

Chaka approached her; he fondled and kissed her and then asked what ailed her. Noliwe answered 'Chaka, my lord, thy brow frowns and thy voice soundeth strained and sorrowful. What hath vexed thee?' Chaka said that nothing had vexed him except that he had been angered by some scoundrel during the drill of his warriors. They continued thus, speaking together happily and exchanging kisses, when suddenly Chaka pressed his strong hand down upon Noliwe's mouth and pierced her with the needle under the armpit. Then he turned her on her side and raised up the part that had been pierced so that the blood might flow back into the wound. When Noliwe was on the point of death her eyelids fluttered a few times and she said: 'Chaka, my beloved, thou who art now my father, who art Jobe, who art Dingiswayo, who art...' the brief candle of her life went out, and her pure spirit fled and went to Dingiswayo to the place of glory above. When Chaka saw her eyelids flutter he was terrified, he began to tremble, and then he fled. When Noliwe was quite dead, Chaka felt within himself something like a heavy stone falling, falling, till it rested on his heart.

He fled outside, but his eyes were dim and he saw nothing, save only the face of Noliwe on the point of death, when her eyelids had fluttered. His ears were stopped, and he heard nothing save only Noliwe's last cry. When he recovered he found himself with Isanusi in the hut and Isanusi was saying words of praise: 'Now thy name hath been enrolled among the number of our chiefs, even the great and the mighty.'

The poor girl who was with Noliwe when Chaka entered was killed; it was said that she had spoken when Noliwe was ill, so that Noliwe died and none knew of it. And Ndlebe spread the report that it was she who had bewitched Noliwe. Isanusi had now taken from Noliwe the thing he wanted to

6-2

take (what it was we do not know), and he prepared it as he alone knew how and the next morning he went with Chaka to the river and Malunga and Ndlebe were there. And when they returned Isanusi made haste to go to his own home.

So died Noliwe, daughter of Jobe, sister of Dingiswayo, and wife of Chaka.

CHUKWUEMEKA IKE

NIGERIA

Too Many Brides

From *Toads for Supper*. This, Chukwuemeka Ike's first novel, is about Amobi, a young man at university in Nigeria whose love affairs get out of hand. He is involved with three different girls, and has promised to marry all of them. Here he is doing his best to back out of one of his promises, a marriage to Nwakaego arranged by his family many years before. But his university training is no match for his father's native wit, an ironic pretence of ignorance which makes Amobi look and feel stupid.

Some days after the party, Mazi Onuzulike again knocked on his son's door. It was 3.45 in the morning. Amobi opened up for him. After preliminary apologies for waking him up so early, his father hit the nail on the head.

'What is it I hear you have been discussing with your mother about Nwakaego?' he asked.

Amobi felt more at home with his mother than with his father; he found it easier to unburden his heart to her first, hear her views before both of them decided whether or not it was worth while taking his problem to his father. And so he had discussed Nwakaego with his mother before retiring for the night. He was surprised that she had spoken so soon to his father about it.

'I don't understand, Sir,' lied Amobi.

'Then everything is all right. I am sorry for disturbing your sleep. Let my words return to me, since what I thought I heard did not happen.' And he made a show of retracing his steps.

'No, Sir…,' faltered Amobi, afraid to let this opportunity slip. 'Nothing has happened, Sir. It's only that I find it difficult to understand one or two things.'

'Like…?'

'Like…whether for instance I must marry Nwakaego?'

Mazi Onuzulike adjusted his heavy, locally woven, white covering cloth and sat down on the chair.

'Who is this Nwakaego you are talking about?'

'That one who comes here,' replied Amobi. 'The daughter of Mazi Nati Ikwuaju.'

'Oh, does she come here? Since when has she been visiting this house?'

'For a long time now.'

'I see.' His father appeared to be thinking. 'Tell me, what does she come here to do? To take fire?'

'No, Sir. If she comes here for fire, the fire would go out before she reaches their house. She comes to visit us, and sometimes to stay for a time to help Mama.'

'How many other girls at Ezinkwo have come to stay with us and help your mother?'

'I can't think of any other.'

'Where is this Nwakaego now?'

'She must be in her father's house,' Amobi replied evasively.

'You must be correct. That did not come to my mind. But tell me, do you remember ever writing to me from the University about this Nwakaego?'

Amobi was becoming more and more uncomfortable about the turn the discussion was taking. He wrinkled his face and narrowed his eyes, in an ostensible effort to recapture past events; his father had given him a long rope.

'I have written so many letters to you and Mama since I left for the University that is is difficult to remember the letter you are referring to.'

'I can well understand. Sometimes I feel sorry for you book people. With all those books on that table inside your small head how can you still have space for small things like the contents of unimportant letters.' He adjusted his covering cloth and produced a crumpled letter which he had hidden away in the folds of the cloth. 'I think this is the letter I have in mind. Perhaps you would like to read it near the light to remember what you wrote in it.'

Amobi's hand was unsteady as he took the letter. He raised the flame of the hurricane lantern, spread out the letter and began to read. His father looked away from him; the gentle tapping of his left foot did not quite synchronize with the gnashing of his teeth. Amobi must have read the letter through at least three times before he returned it to his father.

'Was that the correct letter?' asked his father. 'Old age is affecting me now and I don't know whether I brought the correct letter. Moreover, you know I cannot read.'

For some time neither of them spoke. Amobi turned the contents of the letter over and over in his mind. True, he had in that letter put up a strong case for sending his fiancée, Nwakaego, to the Secondary Modern School. He had, in fact, made it the only condition for marrying her. His father had carried out his instructions in spite of the additional financial burden on a farmer like him. Could he, Amobi, now have any justification for backing out?

'My ears are itching,' remarked his father, in an attempt to break the silence.

'Sir?'

'A proverb has a significance when it falls into the ears of the man who understands; when the good-for-nothing hears it he merely shakes the head till he staggers into the bush. To use proverbs on you young people of nowadays is as futile as running after an antelope. What I said was that I am anxious to hear what you have to say.'

'I have nothing to say, Sir, except that I don't think I shall be happy to marry that girl.'

'Why?'

'Because I don't think she is a suitable match for me.'

Mazi Onuzulike crossed his right leg over the left, gnashing his teeth as was habit in moments of stress. He then spoke slowly.

'My son, you are still young, but not too young. You can now give a woman a child. It is true that the white man's education has brought a new kind of wisdom. We cannot run away from it, just as we cannot run away from the world. We must take what comes in our time. If, however, this white man's learning makes you forget the customs of the father and mother who bore you then it is not good learning.'

He paused to clear his throat. 'Now about Nwakaego. In my own time it was usual for parents to marry wives for their sons. My father was dead even before I tied cloth round my waist, but it was one of my uncles who married a wife for me. I have lived with your mother since then, produced you and trained you to what you are now, and I will continue to train you till you say you have learnt enough book. The Chairman of the Improvement League, Jeremiah the Churchwarden, Mazi Nati Ikwuaju, how can I attempt to count the sand on the ground? They all had wives married for them. Are they not happy with their wives? But the new world is coming; can we run away from it? Osita Umunakwe, in whose house you once stayed at Onitsha, he refused to live with the wife his parents found for him. The day his mother took the girl to him at Onitsha he would have taken them to the charge office, were it not that people intervened to prevent him. He would not give them shelter under his roof even for one night;

it was Nwanneka's husband who gave them food and lodging that night. The following day they returned to Ezinkwo.

'You know what happened. Osita came home to block our ears with talk about a man marrying the girl he loves. We did not know that one bitch as old as his mother had eaten his heart. In spite of every attempt to save the boy from the clutches of these township women who shake their bottoms from one side to another, he fell into the snare like an un-observant grasshopper. Today he is a useless man. After taking away all his money, she has run away to look for another prey. Osita cannot return to Ezinkwo in daylight.

'You know what else happened, only a year ago. Godwin Anagboso nearly died of "small cough". Where is his wife now? Perhaps in Forcados, perhaps in Idah, who knows? Were it not for the advice we gave her, Godwin's mother would have died before her time. Godwin thought that only his eyes could tell which maize was ripe. He thought he knew everything about the girl he wanted to marry, simply because she was a seamstress in the town, a very wicked town, where he was the Local Helper. He was happy he had found a girl who could swell his monthly income of thirty shillings. It was after his wedding in the church that he realised that the wine was not as sweet as the wine tapper made him believe. His wife was wide awake. As soon as she suspected that her husband was losing interest in her, she put some medicine into his soup, and that's why Godwin nearly died of "small cough". She left him last year, without leaving even one child for him.'

Amobi continued to listen. When he looked at his wrist watch his father took the hint.

'The second cock has crowed and I must give you time to snatch a little early morning sleep before day breaks. About Nwakaego. I do not have much to say. One proverb is suffi-cient for a wise man. Nwakaego comes from a good Christian home. Everybody knows that her father and mother have lived happily since they were married. She is a girl everybody likes. I have not heard of her passing any elderly person on the road without saying a word of salutation. She has been brought up very well, and under our own eyes. As you know, she has lived with us for many years of her life and your mother has taken every trouble to train her into a respectful and obedient wife for her son. We know the history of her ancestors which is as good as ours; there has been no trace of madness, white skin, or any other evil disease in their family. Her father and I have been friends from our youth. Her mother and your mother are very good friends. We believe that our children will live happily together.'

Amobi scratched his head at the easy logic.

'You have read more book than any other person, dead or living, at Ezinkwo, for which thanks be to God. If you thank the giver he will give more. I would not ask you to marry someone who has not even heard the schools bells ringing. When you asked me to send Nwakaego to her new school, I agreed to do so even though many people thought I was foolish. I did so without counting the money it would cost me. I did so because I did not want to displease you. I hope you will not do anything that will make me look the daughter of a sheep. Learning is a very good thing, but book learning is not everything. It lies in your hands to turn your wife into whatever you want her to be. Did the daughter of Mgbokwu Anene ever step into a school? Does she not today speak and write English? It needs a hand to turn the forest into a dwelling place. The offspring of a snake cannot be short. A child who resembles neither mother nor father, was it thrown into the compound from the backyard? We know Mazi Nati, we know his wife, we like their ways. Nwakaego is a girl with plenty of commonsense, who is already taking after her mother. If you know you can't marry her because she is not teaching in the

University, tell me. If you prefer those wise girls who help the gods to kill men, and whose family background you know nothing about, to a girl well brought up in a peaceful home, tell me. I have concluded my story and my mouth is tired.'

There was a silence. Amobi held his face in both palms and looked blank.

'My ears are itching,' reminded Mazi Onuzulike. 'You must have something to say, unless you feel I have been throwing up fodder.'

EDWARD BLYDEN
WEST INDIES/LIBERIA

The Pyramids

From *From West Africa to Palestine*. It is not easy to decide whether this passage from Edward Blyden's travel book is intended altogether as seriously as it sounds. Blyden may appear rather solemn, as he makes his large Victorian gestures in heavy, pompous language, but there appears to be a considerable amount of self-mockery here too, which is not surprising since he was a man with a reputation for wit, and a strong sense of the comic. So how are we to take the little scene in which this weighty and serious traveller is pushed protesting up the Great Pyramid by three eager Arabs, one on each side and one to the rear? Or Blyden's stirring appeal from within the centre of the Pyramid to African nationalism and idealism, followed by the refusal of the guides to show him the way out unless he gives them a dash? And what do you make of the last sentence of the extract?

On the morning of the 11th of July, at half-past four o'clock, under the guidance of a young Copt named Ibrahim, I set out for the pyramids. Owing to considerable delay in procuring a boat to cross the Nile—for the pyramids are on the other side of the river from Cairo—we did not reach our destination until eleven o'clock, under a broiling sun.

This journey will long be remembered by me, and will ever be the object of delightful reminiscences. I felt as if I were in an entirely new world. My thoughts were partly of the remote past, but mostly of the immediate future. When crossing the river, an island was pointed out to me as the spot where tradition says Moses was concealed by his mother. My interest was intense.

Half an hour after crossing the river, we caught a view of the pyramids in the distance. Here was opened to me a wide field of contemplation, and my imagination was complete 'master of the situation.' Though we were in an exposed plain, and my companion complained of the intense heat, I did not notice it, so eager was I to gain the pyramids, which seemed further and further to recede the longer we rode towards them. We saw them for three hours before we came up to them.

Just before reaching the pyramids we passed a small village of Arabs, who make their living, for the most part, by assisting travellers to 'do' the pyramids. About a dozen of them rushed out as, they saw us approaching, with goblets of water, pitchers of coffee, candles, and matches, and engraving knives. The water was very acceptable. I looked at the other articles, and wondered what could be the object of them.

The pyramids stand apparently on a hill of sand, on the borders of the Libyan desert. We had to ascend a considerable elevation—about 130 feet— before getting to the pyramid of Cheops. In the side of this apparent hill of sand, extending from the pyramids of Ghizeh to the smaller pyramids of Abusir and Sakarah, about two miles, are excavated tombs. The pyramids are at the extremities of an immense city of the dead, they themselves forming the imperishable tombs of the mighty monarchs who constructed them.

On reaching the base of the great pyramid I tried to find the shady side, but it was impossible to find any shade. On the north side there were several large stones, taken out at the base—leaving huge spaces. Into one of these Ibrahim, myself, and our donkeys entered and sheltered ourselves. The Arabs crowded about us, and kept asking question after question, suggesting the pleasure we should enjoy in ascending to the top, and the advantage to be reaped by visiting the interior. But I paid very little attention to them. They addressed me in broken English, French, and Italian. Other thoughts were crowding my mind. I thought of the continuous fatigue I had undergone, without eating anything, sustained only by the object I expected to attain in front, viz., a close inspection of the pyramids. And now that I had gained my point, I could not help feeling that my effort was, after all, but a forcible type of our experience in one-half of the pursuits we follow through life. My enchanting dreams and fancies left me completely as, heated and weary and hungry, I sat down to rest. How speedily the most cursory experience of the reality often levels to the dust all the mountains built up by the imagination!

After recovering myself by about an hour's rest, I suffered the Arabs to persuade me to ascend the great pyramid (Cheops). Three assisted me; one taking hold of each hand, and one supporting me from behind. Before reaching one-third of the way, however, I gave out, changed my mind, and refused to ascend those dizzy heights. The Arabs clung to me, and insisted that I should go up. I could pacify them only by promising to allow them to take me to the interior—preferring then to examine the interior a little more closely from a less elevated and commanding, but to me a more comfortable, position.

After gazing in amazement at the outside, I made up my mind, in consultation with Ibrahim as to the safety of the enterprise, to visit the central hall in the interior. Had I known, however, that the performance required so much nerve and physical strength as I found out during the experiment, I should not have ventured. The entrance is first by a very steep and narrow passage, paved with immense stones, which have become dangerously slippery by centuries of use. There are small notches for the toes of those who would achieve the enterprise of entering, distant from each other about four or five feet, showing that they were intended for very tall men who wore no shoes. The modern traveller is obliged to make Hiawathan strides to get the toe of his boot into one of these notches, which are also wearing smooth, so as to make the hold which he gets exceedingly precarious. But for the help of these half-naked, shoeless, and sure-footed Arabs, it would be impossible for Western pilgrims generally to accomplish the feat of visiting the interior. Before entering, the Arabs lighted two candles—an operation which, I confess, somewhat staggered me, as it gave me the idea of sepulchral gloom and ghastliness. I had supposed that the interior of the pyramids was lighted in some way, though I had not stopped to think how. As we had to go down sideways, two attended me, one holding my left hand, and the other my right, so that if one slipped the other would be a support. If we had all slipped at once, it is difficult to imagine what would have been the result. The lighted candles were carried in advance.

In about half an hour, after descending and ascending difficult places, we gained the centre. The feeling in going up to the centre of a pyramid is akin to that which one experiences when ascending a very high hill. When we had accomplished the feat of reaching the centre, the Arabs themselves, who are not unaccustomed to the enterprise, seemed to think it a wonderful achievement, for they burst out into simultaneous and boisterous hurrahs. The floor of the hall was one huge stone. On the sides were engraved the names of visitors who had been there centuries ago. But there were very few names: comparatively few travellers, it would seem, go into the pyramids. In the centre of the hall stands the large porphyry coffer in which the embalmed bodies of the kings were deposited— evidently too large to pass through the narrow passages by which we had entered. How was it brought to this place? The Arabs said it was put there while the pyramid was building...

While standing in the central hall of the pyramid I thought of the lines of Teage, the Liberian poet, when urging his countrymen to noble deeds—

> From pyramidal hall,
> From Karnac's sculptured wall,
> From Thebes they loudly call—
> Retake your fame.

This, thought I, is the work of my African progenitors. Teage was right; they had fame, and their descendants should strive, by nobler deeds, to 'retake' it. Feelings came over me far different from those which I have felt when looking at the mighty works of European genius. I felt that I had a peculiar 'heritage in the Great Pyramid'—built before the tribes of man had been so generally scattered, and, therefore, before they had acquired their different geographical characteristics, but built by that branch of the descendants of Noah, the enterprising sons of Ham, from whom I am descended. The blood seemed to flow faster in my veins. I seemed to hear the echo of those illustrious Africans. I seemed to feel the impulse from those stirring characters who sent civilisation into Greece—the teachers of the fathers of poetry, history, and mathematics—Homer, Herodotus, and Euclid... I felt lifted out of the commonplace grandeur of modern times; and, could my voice have reached every African in the world, I would have earnestly addressed him in the language of Hilary Teage—

> Retake your fame!

But I must return from my long digression—which my countrymen, I am sure, will forgive, for the honour of the race—to the interior of the pyramids, looking at which brought on the train of thought which I have indulged.

The heat was not so great within the pyramid as might at first be supposed; it seems to be ventilated from some quarter. Before the Arabs would consent to guide us out they insisted on receiving *bakhshish*—a present, corresponding to *dash* among the aborigines of West Africa. We had to promise them solemnly and earnestly that on gaining the open air we would satisfy all their desires. Had they left us, as they pretended to be about to do, it would have been utterly impossible for us to get out; and the idea of stumbling in the darkness, rolling down slippery places, and falling into deep holes, was harassingly frightful. We were considerably relieved therefore, when they accepted our pledge, and, taking us upon their shoulders, carefully carried us out. And as soon as I breathed once more the pure air I felt how appropriately the words might be written over the narrow entrance, which Dante says he saw inscribed over the gates of everlasting woe:—

Lasciate ogni speranza voi ch'entrate.[1]

On reaching the opening the Arabs sold us coffee, in very small cups, which considerably refreshed us. I felt that my perilous adventure had given me the right of inscribing my name among the hundreds which I saw engraved over and on each side of the entrance, bearing dates as early as the sixteenth century. Borrowing, or rather hiring, for I paid him a shilling for the use of it, an engraving knife from one of the Arabs, I engraved, not far from a name dated 1685, the word LIBERIA, with my name and the date—July 11th, 1866— immediately under it. There is a tolerable degree of certainty, therefore, that the name at least of that little Republic will go down to posterity.

---

[1] 'Give up all hope, you who enter.'

HARRY BLOOM

SOUTH AFRICA

Police Raid

From *Episode*. This novel is about an imaginary racial incident in South Africa. The Africans of a small township have rioted against the White authorities, and the police are making a series of raids on the homes of people suspected of being resistance leaders. But, far from controlling the situation, this only makes matters worse. When this extract begins, Nel, a white police officer with a reputation for brutality has just burst into the home of one of the suspects, Ndimandi.

Nel flung the door open. He was blinded by the sudden light and a moment later was assailed by the warm, sickly air that gushed out of the room. It took him a few seconds to recover. He held his breath and walked in warily, with his revolver drawn and held level with his chest.

All the people in the room were sitting motionless and dead-quiet, staring at the door. Their faces were glistening, and the room reeked of their sweat, and of the uneaten food on the plates that littered the table. There were only men in the room. In the mirror over the sideboard Nel caught a view of the backs of their heads, and then of his own white face and of the bullets gleaming across his chest, and of his men standing behind him.

'Stand up,' he ordered, speaking as if he had an obstruction in his throat.

They all stood up in unison, like children in a classroom. About a third of them seemed to be parsons, and a quarter family elders. It seemed a little queer for a moment. It struck Nel that he had not seen so many turned-around collars and white peppercorn beards in one place in all his life.

'Right,' he said, looking slowly around the room. 'Which one of you's Ndimandi?'

He did not need to be told. Ndimandi was standing in front of the carved chair, supporting himself against the table, and he had a look of such terror in his face that it was impossible to mistake him for anyone else. The other, taller, fat man who was standing beside Ndimandi was Malooy, whom Nel knew.

'You're under arrest,' Nel said, turning the revolver on to Ndimandi. Ndimandi clutched at the side of the table, but otherwise he did not move. The expression on his face did not change; only the colour changed. It changed from deep brown to murky yellow, but the expression remained the same, like that of a wax effigy of himself.

Malooy took a step forward. 'Look, Sergeant,' he said, smiling, 'I think there must be some little mistake.'

'Shut up. Keep out of this, you fat pig. What're you trying to do? Obstruct the police?'

'Sergeant, Sergeant,' Malooy said, coming forward with his palms spread out and smiling genially, 'I'm sure there's a mistake. This man—'

'GET BACK.'

Malooy stopped, his eyes glued on the revolver. His hands dropped to his sides, and he stepped back and stood next to Ndimandi. He was still smiling but the smile had been left stranded on his face, and it looked sick and mirthless against the cold fright that had come into his eyes.

Nel went over to him. He pushed the revolver into Malooy's soft paunch and held it there and stared into his eyes. For more than a minute he stood and stared him out, holding the revolver into the flabby body. Nobody in the room moved. Nel said, 'I'm putting you under arrest, too. For obstructing the police.' He spoke quietly.

Malooy said nothing.

'Stand over there,' Nel said. He moved the gun on to Ndimandi. 'You also.'

Malooy and Ndimandi went over to the corner.

'Turn round.'

They turned and faced into the corner. Nel watched them for a moment, then came back into the centre of the room. 'Right,' he said to the others. 'Form up.'

At first they did not seem to understand what he wanted; maybe they were too stupefied by fright. They looked at him miserably, then at one another, then began to move vaguely around.

'HURRY—damn you. MOVE. HURRY. D'you think I've got all night? Move.' He grabbed a man by the shoulder and sent him hurtling across the room. 'Stand there, you black dog. THERE. Go on, line up from there. ALL of you. From THERE. HERE. For God's sake, HERE.' He was walking about with sharp jerky steps and his rifle was clanking up and down on his back. Sweat was pouring off his face. 'MOVE, you stupid black bastards. LINE UP.' His boot shot out and kicked a man who was passing in front of him. He turned to the other police 'Help me, can't you. Get these black pigs into line. GET INTO LINE. Can't you hear me? Do you want me to bust your faces open?' People were scurrying about, falling over each other and over the furniture. Nel was jabbing the pistol into people's ribs, forcing them into line. 'You black scum, I'll teach you to listen to orders. WELL, MAKE A SECOND LINE, YOU IDIOTS.'

At last they stood in two rows from wall to wall. Nel stepped back and let his eyes travel slowly along the front row. Then he waited. He seemed to be thinking. He was frowning and chewing on the inside of his lower lip.

'Where's the females?' he asked at last, narrowing his eyes. No one answered.

'CAN'T YOU HEAR ME? I ASKED A QUESTION.'

'The women are in the back room, sir,' one of the parsons answered.

'Well, BRING them here. Go on, bring them, and HURRY.'

The man went out of the room into the back part of the house and came back leading the women. They were all wearing black dresses and black veils, and they came down the passage noiselessly, in single file, like a procession of ghosts.

'Here,' Nel said, pointing with the revolver. They lined up facing their menfolk across the room.

'What about the kids?' one of the policemen asked.

'What we want the kids for?' Nel asked.

'There are probably some pretty elderly kids hiding away back there if I know these bastards.'

'O.K.,' Nel said. He turned to the women. 'Where're the kids?'

'The children are sleeping, sir,' a woman said glumly and barely audibly.

'Bring them,' Nel said. 'And hurry.' He ordered two other women to go and help her.

The three women went into the back part of the house and returned with small babies in their arms and a group of older children tailing along behind them. 'Go and see there's no kids with beards and long pants hiding under the beds.' Nel said to his men, and two of them went out and started searching the back rooms.

While the babies were handed out to their mothers, the older children stood rubbing their eyes and scratching their legs and looking back and forth between their elders and the police. They had drugged looks in their faces, and their eyes were milky, as if they had not yet properly awakened from their sleep. Suddenly all the children, the babies in arms and the older children together, started to cry.

'SHUT UP,' Nel shouted. 'Make them shut up,' he said to the mothers. They rocked the small babies against their bosoms, and held the older children under their arms, against their skirts, but it failed to pacify them. Nel became furious. 'SHUT up that bawling,' he bellowed. His voice reverberated through the house. It shocked most of the older children into silence—they stood trembling and tense, but quiet—but the babies went on crying, and then Nel saw that it had been a mistake to bring them out. 'All right, take the small ones back,' he said, and the babies were returned to the back room. They were left there crying, and the women came back and took their places in the line.

Nel turned and faced the men.

'Passes.'

While the men fished in their pockets, pulling out coloured slips of paper, reference books, tax receipts, permits, Nel walked across the room, unhitched his rifle, and handed it to one of his men. Then, wriggling his shoulders and chewing on his lip, he came back and stood before the man who was nearest the wall.

'I see. So you're from Pretoria' he said, examining the man's book.

'Yes, sir.'

'Then what right you got to be in Nelstroom?'

'I came for my cousin's funeral, sir.'

'I said what *right*? Who *told* you you can come to Nelstroom?'

'I got a permit from the superintendent, sir.'

'Let me see it.'

The man handed over his visitor's permit. Nel read it, then held it up to the lamp so that the light shone through. Then he placed his foot on a chair, spread the paper out on his knee, and rubbed his thumb across the signature. He held the paper up to the light again, then held it at arm's length, cocked his head, and squinted at it through one eye.

'It's a forgery,' he said, tearing the document in half.

'No sir, it's not sir, really sir. I saw the superintendent sign it, sir, really, sir,' the man said, almost weeping.

'I say it's a forgery. I don't recognize the signature.'

Nel placed the two halves together and tore them in half, tore the quarters in half, and so on, until the scraps were too small to hold between his fingers. Then he tossed the little bundle of confetti up into the air. 'Arrest him,' he said casually to one of the policemen. The man was handcuffed and taken outside.

Nel took his time examining the rest of the documents. He did not tear up all the permits, only some, as he felt like it. When a document referred to a man's wife or children, he made the wife stand forward and questioned the children about their names and ages to check whether they tallied with the information on the document. He was sharp at finding irregularities—misspelt names, illegible signatures, smudged numbers. He ordered about two-thirds of the men and a third of the women to be arrested. There were not enough hand-cuffs for all the prisoners, so he made them stand under guard out on the pavement. The pickup van driven by the lieutenant from Withoek had returned, and was waiting with its doors open for Nel to come down and start the loading.

When Nel finished examining the documents, he went to the front door, faced round, and said to Ndimandi and Malooy, who were still standing in the corner, 'All right. Turn round. March.'

But as they started to walk towards the door, there was a scream and Ndimandi's wife ran across the room and stood with her arms out in front of her husband.

'He can't go.' Her voice was shrill, almost demented. 'You'll kill him. He's sick. Sick, sick, sick.'

Nel's whole body stiffened. In two huge strides he was in front of her, grappling with her, trying to force her out of the way, but at the same moment Ndimandi darted away from behind her and ran squealing towards the passage that led to the back of the house. Nel let go of her and leapt at Ndimandi, tackling him football fashion and bringing him crashing to the floor. Nel picked himself up and straightened his clothes and said to the remaining policemen in the room:

'O.K. Take him out.'

They picked up Ndimandi by his arms and legs and carried him out face downwards, his face barely clearing the floor. He did not struggle. His body was limp, and they carried him out sagging like a rolled-up carpet.

They took him down into the street, and stood in front of the open doors of the pickup van, swinging him gently back and forth. Nel came out and said, 'Throw him in,' and himself lent a hand to hoist him up. They lifted him shoulder high, and then hurled him clear between the open doors of the empty van. There was a heavy crash, a searing metallic scrape, and a dull thump as his head struck the panel at the far end of the van. There was no other sound.

Now Nel had his revolver out again.

'Right. Now all of you get in.' The other prisoners lined up at the back of the van and began to climb in. A number were inside, including some women, and then there was a wild shriek and they were all back at the door of the van, jumping out into the street. Two women who had been in the van were moaning and screaming and tearing at their clothes. They uttered no words, just raised a shrill hysterical uproar. The men were standing about with their hands at their sides, stunned and frozen.

Nobody dared to look inside the van. Nobody could bring himself to mention Ndimandi's name.

For a moment Nel did not know what to do. He looked helplessly at his men and made futile gestures with his arms, and then Ndimandi's wife came up behind him, and suddenly, before anybody could stop her, pulled a piece of iron pipe from behind her skirt, and, gripping it with both hands, slammed it into the side of his head. He collapsed without a sound, and lay with his head against the wheel of the van. She stood over him, with the iron pipe hanging loosely in her hand, and then she spat at him. But before the spittle ever landed, she herself was dead, shot by a policeman. There was a moment of chilled silence. And then everyone realised that a fight was on, and the stones came flying at the police the same instant as the police started shooting.

MONGO BETI

CAMEROONS

Sports-Day in Kala

From *Mission to Kala*. When the book opens, its hero, Medza, a young Cameroon student, has just failed his *baccalauréat* examination, and returned to his village to face his family's displeasure. But things turn out not so badly, for in spite of his failure and some hard words from his father, his education still makes him a man of importance, and he is soon sent off on a mission to retrieve the wife of one of his cousins from another, even more remote village. Bikokolo, the 'Solomon' of his own village, points out Medza's suitability for the task: 'Shall I tell you what your special thunder is? Your certificates, your learning, your knowledge of white men's secrets. Have you any idea what these up-country bushmen will quite seriously believe about you? That you only have to write a letter in French, or speak French to the nearest District Officer, to have anyone you like imprisoned, or get any personal favour you want. That's the kind of idiocy you'll find waiting for you.'

What I think you might look for here, however, are the elements in the passage which throw doubt on this supposed superiority of Medza. How, for example, do you think that the author expects the reader to react to these words of Medza: 'By what miraculous process, I asked myself, could this man be related to me in any way?' Do we read this as a criticism of Zambo, or an unconscious revelation by Medza of his own arrogance?

I reached Kala about three o'clock in the afternoon. My entry was anything but triumphal—the journey through that hot, dank forest had considerably dampened my enthusiasm and panache—and passed, in fact, almost unnoticed. There was an excellent reason for this; and, indeed, I was at once enlightened as to how far the term 'savage', used that morning by old Bikokolo, was applicable to the local inhabitants.

Just outside the village a remarkable spectacle presented itself to my astonished gaze. It was not the setting which struck me so much as the primitive savagery which animated every participant in the business. There was a sports ground here, a very good one for a mere wattle-and-mud village, and dotted round it were one or two biggish huts, their verandas crowded with spectators anxious to get out of the sun. On the sports ground were about twenty big toughs, bare-legged and bare-chested, engaged in a game whose warlike nature even the Spartans would have recognized. I jumped off my bicycle and wheeled it as close as I could without anyone, performer or spectator, even noticing my presence.

It was baking hot.

Each team consisted of ten or twelve young men lined up in single file, Indian fashion. Thus only the two leaders of each side were actually facing each other, at two or three yards' distance: their supporters backed them up from behind. Each man carried a long, whippy, heavy assegai, its point carefully sharpened. They brandished these weapons in a most dangerous fashion. Right at the end of each file, as far as possible from the captain, that is, stood the strongest man in the team. This man would pick up a ball about the size of a football, made of some hard, heavy, yet porous wood, spin round two or three times like a weight-putter, and throw the ball as hard as he could along the ground. It sped away at a tremendous speed, bumping and bouncing over the rough ground; and as it went the long pointed assegais whizzed out at it so hard and quickly that it was a miracle that no one was hit each time. Often the ball was stopped in mid-flight, pierced clean through by a particularly accurate shot. Then the team's supporters would cheer like mad, and all the lucky marksman's companions smother him with kisses. Then the referee, squatting in one corner of the field, would score five long lines on the ground to the credit of the lucky team. At the end of a match these lines were totted up. When they changed service, so to speak, all the players turned in the same direction—facing the hefty fellow who was going to throw the ball into play, five throws at a time.

I was astonished by the whole thing, though in the end I remembered that when we were about six or so we used to play a similar sort of game at home. But in our case it was a childish pastime, a mere survival from former times, and not taken in the least seriously. At Kala, to judge by this match, it was still going very strong indeed.

From the cheers and shouts of encouragement I gathered that the village of Kala was challenging another village for top place in the league, and that the match I was watching would decide the issue.

Having first taken a bird's-eye, panoramic view of the scene, I now began to examine it in detail. The first thing that caught my eye was a great hulking devil in the Kala team, who had such enormous muscles that I concluded he must have bought them on the instalment system. There was simply no other explanation possible. He was tall and flat-footed, with a disproportionately lengthy torso which, nevertheless, he carried very badly. His buttocks were incredibly slender, yet he retained the country native's slight pot-belly, due to a habitually rough and meagre diet. He was like a kind of human baobab tree. Naturally, he was the one who threw the ball for his team. I had no difficulty in finding out that his name was Zambo: every time he threw the ball the spectators shouted his name in chorus, as though he had been a friendly God to be supplicated at the siege of Troy.

'Zambo, son of Mama!' they yelled, 'Zambo, son of Mama! Zambo! Zambo!'

I found it hard to convince myself that this monster was really my cousin, the young man from whom old Bikokolo had promised me so wonderful a reception. By what miraculous process, I asked myself, could this man be related to me in any way?

When Zambo (son of Mama) wound himself up to 'serve', he shot the ball into play with such force—presumably so as not to favour those of his own team who stood closest to him— that there was very seldom a chance to hit it at all. Generally when an assegai struck the ground, the ball Zambo had thrown had passed by a couple of seconds earlier. Besides, very few of the players in either team made any very serious attempt to hit the ball when this great ape was in charge of it; they were more concerned with getting out of its way. Since they could hardly see it flash by, they preferred to keep clear of it: for them it was a thunderbolt, a divine force both invisible and blind. When Zambo picked up the ball, in fact, it was transformed.

On the other hand, however hard his opposite number 'served', Zambo never flinched from the murderous projectile's path. He watched it hawk-like, dodging round it with fancy footwork, and his shot almost always went home. Then he would clasp his hands above his head like a boxer and himself yell: 'Zambo, son of Mama!' as if to proclaim his victory.

I still remember one extraordinary incident which brought most of the spectators to their feet with exclamations of horror. The ball, pitched on this occasion by the opposition, was whizzing towards the Kala team at a really colossal speed. They all gave it a pretty wide berth, as though it were a charging rhino—all, that is, except Zambo, who stood his ground, bounding about like a huge antelope and squaring up to his target with truly heroic sang-froid. But in the split second before the ball reached him, it either hit a stone or some ridge in the ground, and shot up into the air. It rose so sharply that it would have knocked Zambo's head off (he was a very tall man) if he hadn't ducked like a flash. Even in this crisis he still found time to fling his assegai into the air. I don't know exactly what happened; I shut my eyes at the crucial moment and, anyway, it was all over in an instant. But when I dared look again, the sports ground was echoing with the frantic cheers of all the spectators. The ball lay at Zambo's feet, pierced clean through; and Zambo himself was glaring at it, as though hypnotizing it into yet humbler submission.

The whole match was a kind of Zambo benefit; it was not the Kala team that won, but Zambo on his own. I was proud of my cousin, but nevertheless felt an instinctive fear and re-pugnance at the very sight of him—perhaps because the weak are naturally terrified by strength and therefore come to hate it. The temporary Conquistador in me suddenly decided that it was far preferable to be a ploughed student again. All I wanted to do at that moment was get back into my ordinary clothes and put my best suit away in the wardrobe again.

The sun was sinking behind the forest ridge like a scuttled and blown-up ship, and at last the match came to an end. The twenty young men were completely exhausted, especially after having played tag for so long with that lethal ball, in a kind of endless dance. Zambo left the field escorted by a crowd of boys singing patriotic hymns (or something of the sort) and several girls, who kept up an ear-splitting series of triumphal war-whoops. Like a young god he marched proudly past me, and I stood there, petrified.

Yet after he had moved on, for some inexplicable reason he turned and looked back: our eyes met. His gaze lingered on me, and he knitted his brows thoughtfully. Then he turned away and moved off with his escort again, but almost at once turned back for a second time. After a moment's hesitation he came over to me. It was only then that his attendants became aware of my presence, and took in the fact that I was dressed like a townsman and was wheeling a magnificent bicycle.

My athletic cousin was the first to break the silence, in some evident confusion. He could hardly have been more confused than I was.

'I cannot help thinking I know you,' he said.

'It would not surprise me to hear it.' I tried to make my voice sound dignified. Dignity was the one advantage I had left.

'But it is probable that you, on the other hand, do not know me,' Zambo went on. 'The circumstances in which we have met before have always been unfavourable to your making my real acquaintance.'

'Really?' I said. 'Where would that have been?'

'It's too long a story. Townsfolk like you hardly ever bother to get to know your relations. With us it's different.'

I said: 'You are Mama's son, though aren't you? David Mama, that is?'

'Yes, indeed. Your cousin, and at your service.'

'At my service?'

'Little cousin,' Zambo said, 'you can't imagine how delighted and honoured I am to be able to talk to you today. You can have no idea—'

Delighted and honoured? To talk to *me*? I couldn't understand it. I must have misheard him. My athletic cousin did not, however, sound as though he were joking. For a moment I really believed I was going to faint with shock. There stood Zambo, smiling benignly at me and exposing all his magnificent teeth: benevolent, friendly, fraternal, even a little obsequious. His whole attitude was exactly what was needed to reassure me completely; yet somehow reassurance failed to come. Try to imagine a poor insignificant creature, an ex-Conquistador retreating (after a brief career) in some confusion, a mere failed student once more, who is confronted with the spectacle of a young god falling down at his feet and worshipping him. For a moment I hated my cousin. I resented this unexpected reversal of our roles, and the way in which, for the third time that day, I had been forced to revise my estimate of my own strength.

Besides, Zambo was not alone in his disconcerting attitude. All the young boys and girls who had been singing *his* praises now turned and clustered round *me*, displaying the indiscriminate admiration and generally unrestrained behaviour which (I supposed) were only to be found among such up-country bushmen.

'Look at his clothes,' one said. 'He's a proper town boy, isn't he?'

'Oh, he's a town boy all right. Look at that bike. What a swell he must be!'

'Good-looking, don't you think?'

'*And* young.'

I felt most embarrassed. I wanted to tell them that I wasn't a swell at all, and nearly as old as my cousin Zambo, their champion. But this first experience of such imbecile admiration paralysed me. I had been brought up for six years or more to believe in modesty, even on occasion humility, and I was beginning to resent their attentions. Zambo (who continued to grin obsequiously at me) must in the end have noticed my embarrassment, for he invited me home to get a little rest, as he put it. I accepted thankfully. He insisted on pushing the bicycle.

While we walked, with our common fans stretched out behind us like a pack of hounds that has picked up an unexpected scent, Zambo asked me why I had come to Kala.

I gave him a brief account of the affair, and told him—with careful emphasis—that I was to stay with his father, if this was not inconvenient. When I mentioned this caveat, Zambo looked as astonished as if his grandmother (who had died ten years earlier) had suddenly materialized in front of him and asked, very humbly, for a drink.

'But, little cousin,' he protested, 'we should be highly honoured to have you in our house, naturally—the pleasure is all ours—'

Honoured again. What did it all mean? At this point he launched into a long rambling speech of which I remember only the essential point, which was that everyone ought to show me great respect because of my learning and diplomas. I reflected that my family back home had seen the matter in a rather different light.

ADEROGBA AJAO

NIGERIA

Twisting the Lion's Tail

From *On the Tiger's Back*. This book is an account by a Nigerian student of a period of studies in Eastern Europe at a Communist-controlled university. In the end, he found that life there suited him even less than it did in Britain, but it was in Britain that he first developed the sympathy for Communism that was to take him to Eastern Europe. In this extract, he has just left Edinburgh and come down to Leicester, and he tells of student life there.

When I went to Leicester I was beginning to feel my manhood strong upon me. I had seen life, I had heard new ideas. I was no longer the schoolboy from Lagos, who knew nothing. I knew something about life, and I had shed illusions. And I thought I knew what I wanted. There was still my obsession about technical training, technical wisdom, which would give me the secret of fortune and at the same time enable me to help my country to shake off foreign rule and bring itself out into the world, into a world in which it would not survive without industrialization.

Looking back, I can see that I had a pretty naïve set of notions, but the central proposition was not wrong. It wasn't wrong then and it isn't wrong now. But I probably thought the whole thing was easy, if only I could find out the secret.

One of the courses I took at Leicester was on economics. I thought that economics was the study of economic and industrial development. I expected to learn how to run an industry, how to run a business, how to assess the swing of prices, how, in other words, to be successful and make money. Economic theory, the economic classics, was not what I really wanted. I remember in one lecture hearing a long disquisition about the fluctuations of markets, including stock market values. I asked the lecturer a question: 'I have heard your lecture with interest, but why have you not told us how to predict these fluctuations? What is the use of learning the theory of these matters if it cannot be used to predict events?' The class laughed at me, and the lecturer explained that however sound economic theories, there were imponderables in so many aspects of the business that prediction could not be accurate and it was better not to indulge in it.

I could see that I had expected too much, but the point rankled. Surely there must be some practical way of treating these matters in a purely materialistic way, and getting a workable answer.

In Leicester I stayed in one of the Halls of Residence. This was much more satisfactory than the hostel in Edinburgh, because here there was no question of being tucked away in a polite sort of colonial ghetto, cut off from the rest of humanity. The mixture was complete. There were Africans and Asians and Arabs and West Indians, as there had been in Edinburgh, but there were also English, Welsh, Scots and all the rest of them. I was glad I had changed horses, and was prepared to work and to enjoy myself.

It was only after I had lived and tried to study in Eastern Europe under a Communist régime that I realized how sharp is the contrast between a country, like Britain, where no authority even suggests that a student should interest himself in politics, and a Communist country where an interest in politics is inescapable, obligatory, even if it is in a political theory and practice of a particular type to the exclusion of all others.

I was interested in politics in Leicester because I wanted to be, because I *was* deeply interested, because it was part of my need in life, an essential part of my nourishment as a human being. There were plenty of students who were not interested in politics in Leicester, who wanted no part of it. But to me, politics, and talk about political issues, were essentials, and anyone who wanted to talk politics would find no difficulty in getting me to join in.

As a lonely student, with no particular ties, I looked round various student organizations in order to see which would suit me best. All the political parties were organized, except that I think the Communist Party which had once been organized within the college had been kicked out or had faded out.

The Labour Party was in power in Britain at that time. It now strikes me as strange that with all my curiosity about politics, with my natural instinct for the Left because the Right, in relation to Nigeria, could not possibly have drawn me to it, I was never for a moment attracted to the British Labour Party. I read about it, of course, and heard people talk about it, but never for a moment did it have the slightest appeal for me. I accepted the idea, which was universally accepted, within my acquaintance by colonial students, that

Labour Party policies for the colonies were, for all practical purposes, the same as those of the Conservative Party. If they said otherwise, they did not mean it. If they meant otherwise the 'imperialists' would prevent them putting their policies into effect. I recognize that this was all very unfair to the Labour Party, but the fact remains that it never managed to appeal to us.

My absorption in politics grew and, I have no doubt, did my college studies little good. I read everything; I haunted the Leicester Public Library when I should no doubt have been haunting the college library, I read fat books about the industrial development of the United States, of Japan, of the Soviet Union. I read about Hitler's rise to power. Who had the secret? Was it Hitler, perhaps? Maybe he had been right in many ways about the economy of Germany, and went astray and was destroyed for the wrong reasons. What lessons could I learn from all this for myself and for Nigeria? I was biting off a good deal more than I could chew, but fortunately did not know it.

I had not been many months in Leicester when my political awakening began to take on a more recognizable pattern. My reading had included Edgar Snow's *Red Star Over China*, a book beyond measure exciting, and available in the Leicester Public Library, but not in the college library. There was the *Daily Worker* which seemed to be saying all the right things about the colonies writhing under the heel of the imperialists. I read, and I talked. And I got more pleasure from talking to people who agreed with me than with those who didn't.

It was in this way that I first came across the Young Communist League. Looking back on these earnest young people after my life under the disciplines of a Communist State, I can see how lightly indoctrinated they were. There was dogmatism, and a faith in the ultimate rightness of the Marxist-Leninist-Stalinist thesis, but there was a willingness to admit the existence (although not the ultimate validity) of other ideas in a way which was quite out of the question for their contemporaries in Eastern Europe.

Apart from the sympathy I had for their point of view there was also the fact that the Young Communists were very friendly to me, and seemed to take my African-ness in their stride. They never laughed at my ideas about the regeneration of the world and the advancement of the people of Africa as others sometimes did in a rough and ready, but seldom malicious, way. I made friends with them. I went to their houses.

They seemed to have the right ideas, and above all they had a kind of certainty about the rightness, and the ultimate victory, of their point of view, which was exactly what I sought. In the welter of ideas which prevail in an intellectually unrestricted society, it is probably seldom realized how very disconcerting and unsatisfying the apparent absence of fixed political theories can be. A seeker after political foundations, in British society, is like a child whose parents take to extremes the notion that a child is not to be frustrated and must never be compelled to do what he does not want to do. Such a child is often unhappy, and uncertain, with nothing firm to cling to, nothing to save him from ceaseless uncertainty.

This notion was one of the factors which led me towards Communism: certainty. It was immensely attractive, and many a time, in the countless discussions in which I took part during this period, privately, with individuals, or later, in the more organized occasions arranged by the Young Communist League, my own doubts were swamped by the Communist argument that even if certain phenomena did not seem to fit into the prescribed pattern that was only because one saw them from the wrong angle, through the distorting lens of bourgeois thinking, or because, unhappy wretch that I was, I had been brought up under alien domination.

And there was Jean. Jean was about eighteen. She worked in an office. And she was treasurer of one of the Leicester groups of the Young Communist League. Jean was a nice friendly sort of girl who liked talking about politics, and she devoted her young fervours to Marxism-Leninism in much the same way as some of her less intelligent contemporaries devoted theirs to clothes or dancing.

There were quite a lot of people like Jean about in Leicester and I suppose also in other towns of the same sort in England. However deluded they may have been about the Soviet Union's domestic history or about its intentions towards the non-Communist world, these young people were probably sincerely attached to certain perfectly respectable ideals. They believed that the world could be improved and that it was worth making an effort to improve it. And, what is more, they felt it their duty to make the effort themselves. They got pleasure from the conviction that the society in which they lived was a bad one and that there were abuses that could be removed. And in post-war British society there were many things that needed attention. Parliamentary democracy in Britain failed to appeal to young people who were in general among the 'have nots' and when the Communist Party told them firmly that the solution was easy and was one that they could help to work out, there was no reason why they should not believe it.

The main trouble with foreign students in England at that time was that there was not enough for them to do, and they had not enough money for the kind of amusements such as Leicester offered, like picture-houses or pubs. So the Students' Club or the coffee houses became their meeting ground and their endless hours were spent on talk.

There was one Leicester club in particular where we used to meet. It was an international club set up mainly for students by some philanthropic body with no political attitudes, but it was, in fact, the place where political ideas were discussed at length and where sundry plots were hatched. It always amused me to think that the kindly sponsors of the club probably believed that its existence kept students' minds off mischievous political notions when in fact—what with the unreadable books provided and our inability to devote our whole time to playing table-tennis—we expended all our surplus energy in trying to bring about the doom of the imperialists, colonialists and capitalists in whose world, although not exactly in whose bosom, we were living.

The master-mind of the group was an Iraqi student who was eventually sent away from England by his own government whose patience with his ability to create trouble and to get mixed up in what seemed to them undesirable political activities became exhausted. Salek was one of those dynamic characters with an enormous amount of energy and an endless flow of argument against all the Communist targets. When he was launched on a diatribe against British imperialism in the Middle East, or the terrible miseries of the capitalist system, nothing could stop him, and his eloquence was very persuasive. But Salek was no mere talker: he had all sorts of ideas about political action and he had his eye on the future.

Not far from Leicester there was a military training establishment, at Loughborough. Among the trainees there were some Pakistanis. It was Salek's idea that we should get in touch with those Pakistanis when they came to Leicester to taste its social joys. It was not so much that he wanted to subvert them or to induce them to blow up their training establishment. He simply wanted to identify them, make himself known to them on the assumption that people trained in this way might return to Pakistan and eventually occupy positions in the Pakistan Army of comparative power. The time might come, if a revolutionary situation developed in Iraq, when the contact could be usefully renewed.

It sounds fantastic now. But was it so fantastic? There have been military *coups d'état* in both Iraq and Pakistan and one of them was accomplished by officers who got some if not all of their inspiration, not to speak of active aid, from the Communists.

As a member of the Young Communist League in Leicester I attended many of their meetings and drank their coffee as the gatherings moved from house to house. These meetings varied. Sometimes there were members only: sometimes the members brought friends. When the formal talks ended the discussions which followed would take for granted fewer Communist propositions and encourage an attitude of sweet reasonableness, permitting the holding of diverse views. It was by these means that the Young Communist League kept up its numbers because there was a certain amount of wastage in the membership. Young men and women drifted in and out, drifting out if they were only half-in intellectually when they found something more amusing to do or perhaps when they got a higher wage.

Occasionally some of us got involved with local politics when we helped candidates seeking election to municipal councils. These candidates were not necessarily Communists but could belong to any part of the Left or centre, preferably as Left as possible. I do not remember that we ever succeeded in getting any of our candidates in but it merely convinced us of the rightness of our cause, and the blindness, stupidity, and wickedness of everybody else. We knew, and we were happy in the knowledge, that a great cause demands its martyrs and that we were in the vanguard of a heroic struggle against the Titans.

I lived for about a year in the hostel at Leicester. It was a reconditioned nineteenth-century villa, so I was told, and I had to take the fact on trust since I had no particular eye for the finer points of architecture. It was big, anyway, and it stood in Glenfield Road on the outskirts of the town. There were about a dozen students off and on, for they came and went.

When I try to recall exactly who they were and in what proportion of nationalities, I find that my arithmetic never quite works out. I suppose that those who made the deepest impression on me may only have seemed to be there all the time, and those I never particularly noticed were there all the time.

The place was well run, with rules only stringent enough to keep it in working order. All the students came from my college. There was a housekeeper who managed the place, and there were cleaners. Most of us had to share a room, but there was plenty of space, considering everything, and after all students have no special claim to live in luxurious conditions. There was a lounge, I remember, with leather armchairs. We all had breakfast in the hostel, but not a midday meal. This we had at college, or in a café somewhere, or we had none. And we had supper, or dinner, or whatever it was called, again at the hostel. The meals weren't bad, although at the price we paid (£2 to £3 a week) they were not very exciting. Good and plain, and the foreigners had to accept that they were on an English diet and there was not much they could do about it. We could not afford to pay for the hostel and eat meals out as well.

There was a real attempt to make the hostel work smoothly. We had our meals at separate tables, or at any rate not at one big central table, so that we could choose our companions if we wanted to. And the place was clean. Altogether, there wasn't much to complain about in the purely material sense, in the villa in Glenfield Road. The dissatisfaction and boredom, and the search for escape and inspiration, were not a direct outcome of either unsympathetic or physically uncomfortable surroundings, and it is difficult to see what else could have been done, except perhaps to show some realization that a collection of students from countries in political ferment, or about to be, would find some sort of outlet somewhere. I suppose that, in a country like England, the notion of leaving people to find their own salvation without any attempt to direct them is too ingrained to change. But it produces some funny results. I have often wondered about this, this English *knowing* what works (giving them the benefit of the doubt for the moment) but thinking it is self-evident and not worth the bother of explaining or of persuading other people to adopt it. But I must not start wondering about it now.

Of the ten or a dozen students there at various times, I recall that there were usually between three and five English or Scottish or Welsh natives. There were two Nigerians, of whom I was one. My fellow Nigerian was from Lagos, and had a scholarship. He sniffed around political matters like a dog afraid of getting bitten. There was one Cameroonian. The main thing I remember about him was that he was always complaining about the cold. He was a Civil Servant who had come to England to get a qualification which would give him a step up in the administration. He was not what could fairly be called politically simple, but I think the Civil Servant part of him was on the top, and he had no wish to involve himself in the discussion of large political ideas or their possible effects. There were six Iraqis, one Israeli (that is, then, a Palestinian), one Eurasian Malay and one Indian.

My room-mate for some time was an English grammar-schoolboy. Atkins was his name. He was perfectly amiable, but I could never get a spark of politics out of him. He was in fact a conventional standard-pattern English student, who wanted to get on with his studies, and who obviously thought that an interest in politics was all very well for a lot of slightly dubious foreigners, who couldn't be expected to know about these things by instinct, and therefore had to be arguing about them all the time instead of getting on with their education.

In the hostel, in the evenings, we used to find ourselves

trying to fill up the gap between dinner and bedtime. Often the atmosphere, for those of us who were far away from home, was dull to a painful degree. We should have been studying, no doubt, but we preferred to talk. In situations like that there is always someone who takes the lead. Usually it was the Iraqi. He was an urbanized middle-class type—it would have been difficult for him to get to England to study if his family had not had means. He regarded himself as a genuine Marxist, but an impure one.

Heresy, so intolerable to the true Stalinist of the period, was widespread among foreign students, and among the indigenous variety in Britain too—that one could be a Communist with reservations, a Communist with national prejudices, a Communist who was prepared to see some good in some of the things that went on in hopelessly un-Marxist countries like Britain.

What really made Salek tick was anti-imperialism, which for him meant outside influence on Iraq and other Middle East countries where Western Europeans had an interest and expressed it by various forms of control and interference. It was against British influence that Salek came out strongest. At the same time, he admired England for many things. I often met with this sort of thing, and certainly could have watched it going on in my own mind.

It is perfectly possible to admire a country and its people and its institutions, and at the same time to hate it passionately, to wish for its destruction, to wish to see its self-satisfied smile wiped off its fat red face. I have heard all kinds of fancy attempts, by anthropologists and political and social analysts, to explain this double attitude, to go into it as if it was something mysterious and inexplicable. To my mind there is nothing particularly mysterious about it. What else could be expected? The English should be familiar with it, if anyone should be. The class structure in England is really very like the relationship between foreign rulers and dependent peoples. Many Nigerians read the writings of H. G. Wells, who depicted very well certain kinds of social resentment. Whenever that social resentment becomes even slightly sophisticated, which is probably just as soon as the idea is generated that human relations are not permanent and can be changed, what was formerly acquiescent, and even in some cases genuine, gratitude to the superior being gives place to the desire for radical change and a deep dislike of the benefactor.

Britain occupies a curious position in all this. The very indifference to criticism—especially from foreign students—preserved a kind of reluctant respect. There is respect, too, for the British system of giving living space and education to thousands of foreign students and at the same time leaving them to their own devices when it could be influencing their political attitudes. It is one of the ironies of history that so many revolutionaries should have learnt their philosophies in the countries whose interests they set out to destroy. The Indonesians who were to form the new republic after the war learned their liberal and 'progressive' ideas in the universities of the Netherlands. The Indo-Chinese learned theirs at the Sorbonne or in the cafés with Thorez. The Indians and West Africans licked their political ice-cream in the London School of Economics and, somehow, in the Inns of Court.

THE AUTHORS AND THEIR BOOKS

The books listed here are those with African backgrounds, and so in some cases not all the works of an author are included.

PETER ABRAHAMS was born in Johannesburg in 1919. His father was an Ethiopian and his mother a Cape Coloured. He was educated at St Peter's College and left South Africa in 1939, spending two years as a seaman. He then settled in Britain until 1957, since when he has lived in the West Indies. He is at present Editor of the *West Indian Economist*. Publications include: *Mine Boy* (1946), *Path of Thunder* (1952), *Wild Conquest* (1951), *Tell Freedom* (1954), *Return to Goli* (1953), *Jamaica, An Island Mosaic* (1957), *A Wreath for Udomo* (1956), *A Night of Their Own* (1965).

CHINUA ACHEBE was born in Ogidi, Nigeria, in 1930. He graduated at Ibadan, spent some time in London with the B.B.C. and is at present Director of External Broadcasting at the N.B.C., Lagos. Publications: *Things Fall Apart* (1958), *No Longer at Ease* (1960), *Arrow of God* (1964), *A Man of The People* (1966).

MOTOLANI ADEROGBA AJAO was born at Awe-Ojo, Nigeria, in 1930, and educated in Lagos, at George Watson's College, Edinburgh, at the Leicester College of Technology and Commerce, and at Leipzig University in East Germany. He is at present an industrial consultant in Nigeria. Publication: *On the Tiger's Back* (1962).

EDWARD ATIYAH was born in the Lebanon in 1903, and educated in Alexandria and at Oxford University. He worked in Khartoum from 1926 to 1945, first as a lecturer in History, but after one year as Government Public Relations Officer. He has been in London since 1945, as Secretary to the Arab Office, and later, as Press Adviser to the Iraqi Embassy. Publications include: *An Arab Tells His Story* (1946), *The Thin Line* (1951), *Black Vanguard* (1952), *The Arabs* (1955), *The Eagle Flies from England* (1960), *Donkey for the Mountains* (1961).

SOLOMON ATTOH-AHUMA changed his surname from Solomon to Attoh-Ahuma at a time when this was a common protest against English domination in Africa. He was Editor of the *Gold Coast Methodist Times*, which under his editorship took on an increasingly political tone and was of great importance in encouraging Gold Coast nationalism. Objections to this tone led to his resignation and the journal's failure shortly after. He joined the staff of another journal, *The Gold Coast Aborigines*, in which his political writing was continued, and he was also one of the leaders of the Gold Coast Aborigines' Rights Protection Society. He died in 1922. Publications include: *Memoirs of African Celebrities* (1905), *The Gold Coast Nation and National Consciousness* (1911).

MONGO BETI was born in the Cameroons in 1930, and educated locally, and at the Sorbonne in Paris. Two of his novels are available in translations by Peter Green—*Mission Terminée* and *Le Roi Miraculé* published under the titles *Mission to Kala* (1958) and *King Lazarus* (1960). Another novel, *Le Pauvre Christ de Bomba* (1956) is not yet translated.

HARRY BLOOM was born in Johannesburg in 1913 and educated at the University of Witwatersrand. He is a lawyer by profession. Publications include: *Episode* (1956), *Sorrow Laughs* (1959), *Whittaker's Wife* (1962). He also wrote the book of the African jazz opera *King Kong* (1961).

EDWARD W. BLYDEN was born in St Thomas, West Indies, of Togoland parents, in 1832. He went to the United States while still a boy, and from there to Liberia, where he had a distinguished career as a scholar and diplomat. He became President of Liberia College, Monrovia, in 1880, and Liberian Minister in London in 1892. He died in 1912. Publications include: *Liberia, Past Present and Future* (1862), *The Negro in Ancient History* (1869), *From West Africa to Palestine* (1873), *Christianity, Islam and the Negro Race* (1887), *Africa, and the Africans* (1903), *West Africa before Europe* (1905), *African Life and Customs* (1908).

DRISS BEN HAMED CHARHADI was born in Morocco in 1939. He can neither read nor write, and his book is an oral narrative in Moghrebi Arabic. He works as a cook and general servant.

HARRY DEAN was born in the United States in 1864, a descendant of the negro traveller Captain Paul Cuffee. He travelled widely as a merchant seaman, being deported from Africa for his support of African nationalism. *Umbala*, in the writing of which he was assisted by Sterling North, was published in 1929.

CYPRIAN EKWENSI was born in 1921 in Nigeria, and educated in Nigeria and Ghana. He trained as a pharmacist in London, but gave up pharmacy as a career in order to devote more time to writing. He was in charge of Feature Programmes at the Nigerian Broadcasting Corporation, but left this post to become Director of Information for the Federal Government in Lagos. Publications include: *People of the City* (1954), *Jagua Nana* (1961), *Burning Grass* (1962), *Beautiful Feathers* (1963).

WAGUIH GHALI was born in Egypt in 1935, and his background is much like that of Ram and Font, the principal characters of his novel. He left

Egypt some years ago after a disagreement with the Egyptian government over some articles he wrote criticizing their foreign policy. He now lives in West Germany. Publications include: *Beer in the Snooker Club* (1964).

CHUKWUEMEKA IKE was born in Eastern Nigeria in 1931. He is a graduate of Ibadan, and is now Registrar at the University of Nsukka. Publication: *Toads for Supper* (1963).

JOMO KENYATTA was born in Kenya in 1889. He was educated at the London School of Economics, and was President of the first Pan-African Congress. As leader of the Kenyan African Union he was in prison or detained from 1952 to 1961, and is now Prime Minister of Kenya. Publications include *Facing Mount Kenya* (1938), *My People of Kikuyu* (1942), *Kenya, Land of Conflict* (1945), *Harambee!* (Speeches) (1965).

PETRO KILEKWA was born in Northern Rhodesia (now Zambia) about 1875. He was captured by Arab slavers, but after his release, described in this episode, he became a seaman in the Royal Navy. He remained behind when his ship was posted back to Britain, and entered Kiungani College, Zanzibar, to train as a missionary, and afterwards served for many years in Nyasaland. His autobiography, *Slave Boy to Priest*, translated by K. H. Nixon Smith, was published in 1937.

THOMAS MOFOLO was born in Basutoland in 1887 and worked there as a teacher and as a clerk in a book depot, and later in the gold mines. He ended up owning a store. His three books were written in Sotho. He died in 1948. Publications include: *Chaka, An Historical Romance*, translated by F. H. Dutton (1931), *The Traveller of the East*, translated by H. Ashton (1934).

JAMES NGUGI was born in Kenya in 1940. He was educated at Makerere and afterwards as a post-graduate student at Leeds University. He has written one play, *The Black Hermit*, and two novels have been published, *Weep Not, Child* (1964) and *The River Between* (1965).

ABIOSEH NICOL is the pen-name of a distinguished West African scholar and scientist. Publications include: *Two African Tales* (1965), and short stories by him can be read in several anthologies—P. Rutherfoord's *Darkness and Light*, L. Hughes's *An African Treasury*, P. Edwards's *West African Narrative* and *Modern African Narrative*.

JOHN E. OCANSEY was one of the sons of William Narh Ocansey, a general merchant of Addah in Ghana and brother to the chief of Addah. He was an adopted son, and formerly a slave in the Ocansey household, but subsequently married one of the Ocansey daughters. In 1880, John went to represent the family in a lawsuit to be heard in London, against an English company which owed his father over £2,000. He discusses the lawsuit and also gives a description of his English experiences in his book, *African Trading; or the Trials of William Narh Ocansey* (Liverpool, 1881). He died in 1889.

WILLIAM PLOMER was born in South Africa in 1903, and now lives in Britain. Publications include: *Turbott Wolfe* (1926), *I Speak of Africa* (1927), *Paper Houses* (1929), *Cecil Rhodes* (1933), *The Child of Queen Victoria* (1933), *Double Lives* (1940), *Four Countries* (1949), *Collected Poems* (1960).